Visceral Magick

Bridging the Gap Between Mundane and Magick

Peter Paddon

Visceral Magick

Bridging the Gap Between Mundane and Magick

Peter Paddon

PENDRAIG Publishing
Los Angeles, CA 91040

Visceral Magick - Bridging the Gap Between Mundane and Magick
By Peter Paddon
First Edition © 2010
by PENDRAIG Publishing

Edited by   Tony Mierzwicki

Cover Design & Interior Images
Typeset & Layout   Jo-Ann Byers Mierzwicki

PENDRAIG

PENDRAIG Publishing
Los Angeles, CA 91040
www.PendraigPublishing.com
Printed in the United States of America

ISBN: 978-0-9843302-3-2

Dedication

To my wife Linda,
for putting up with my crap...
and for the love we share.

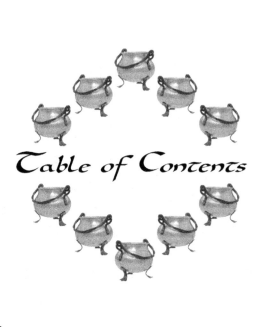

Table of Contents

Introduction

Over the last ten or twelve years, I have found my spiritual journey has taken on a few unusual twists. Before that, I was an Alexandrian Wiccan living and working in England – though I already knew that I wanted to find something deeper, darker and stronger. I had already experienced what has become a recurring theme in my life, where I have a personal internal experience that provides me with information that is later verified through research. Back in 1984, in the pursuit of the Egyptian Mysteries, I had connected with an entity who offered to teach me. He told me his name was Amenemta, and that he had been the High Priest of Ra at the Temple of Abydos in the reign of Seti I. This seemed very strange at the time, because Abydos was the cult center for Osiris, King of the Underworld and Judge of the Dead. You can imagine my surprise when I discovered that because Abydos has seven sanctuaries, one of which is dedicated to Ra Herachty, there was indeed a High Priest of Ra at that temple, and during the reign of Seti I and partway through the reign of Ramses II, this role was held by a man called Amenemta (also written as Amenemhet or Amenhotep), who was also Chief of Works – another fact the entity had told me about himself.

Fast-forward a few years, and in 1997 I moved to Los Angeles, and began training with Roebuck coven, under Ann and Dave Finnin [Ancient Keltic Church, Clan of Tubal Cain, 1734]. This training was the perfect transition from the Wiccan way of doing things, so that in 2000, when I encountered Wildewood coven, headed by Raven Womack, I was ready to embrace what was to become my true spiritual path. The thing that has marked my journey since then has been the ever-increasing physicality of my interaction with the more subtle realms. I have come to refer to this physicality as Visceral [the dictionary definition of visceral is 1. Of or relating to the viscera, or 2. Relating to deep inward feelings rather than to the intellect: "the voters' visceral fear of change".] Magick, because it began with a "gut-reaction" to the energy of sacred space, a very physiological response, as I began to notice that the energy of a rite would literally make the hairs on my arms and the back of my neck stand up.

I didn't have any framework or validation to my experiences, but as the visceral or physiological component became stronger, I began to have experiences that reinforced the effect, as well as provided a backdrop where they made sense. I began looking for a model on which to build a picture of my experiences, and rediscovered the Cauldrons of Poesy, an Irish Celtic poem that expressed a concept generally believed to be universal across the Celtic world, that of the Three Cauldrons.

Working with the Three Cauldrons in much the same way as a ceremonial magician might work with the spheres of the Tree of Life or the Hindu Chakras, as energy centers within the body, I found that this focused and strengthened the visceral effect yet again, and I began to notice that this visceral way of crafting seemed not to need the conscious focus and concentration of the crafting I'd done before... it was as if another intelligence was taking its cue from my physical efforts and completing the crafting for me.

Shortly after I realized that my magick was invoking the aid of another intelligence that was still somehow me, I stumbled upon the recent work in the medical field concerning visceral intelligence. It appears that there is ample evidence to suggest that the lower digestive tract, intestines, colon and bowel, contain a neural network that is responsible for the autonomic reactions of the gut, rather than those involuntary actions being under the control of the brain. Doctor Michael Gershon, regarded as the father of modern neurogastroenterology, rediscovered the work of two Victorian scientists, Bayliss and Starling. Working in labs at Oxford University, they discovered that many of the autonomic functions of the gut are controlled by a nexus of neurons in the intestines, rather than by the brain. They discovered this after one of them took a section of living bowel from a dog (kept alive in a dish filled with nutrients) and blew into it. To their surprise, the bowel section blew back! It turns out that between the two walls of muscle that encircle the tube that is our digestive tract lies a nexus of neurons that operate in the same way as the neurons of the brain. A great deal of practical experimentation had led researchers to the rediscovery of something taken for granted by our Celtic ancestors – that the human gut contained an intelligence that could work independently of the brain and respond to physiological and emotional stimuli. It turns out that the "gut-feeling" we all have from time to time was an example of this in everyday life.

So that validated – for me at least – the Cauldron of Warming in the gut (as described in the poem), and the Cauldron of Wisdom in the head speaks for itself, but it made me wonder about the Cauldron of Motion in the heart, though I did not have to wonder for long. I shared my thoughts on the subject to my brother Colin [Colin Paddon Ph.D., D.Ac., D.N.M. is a Doctor of Traditional Chinese Medicine and Naturopathic Medicine. He is a gifted healer, and one of Canada's foremost teachers of holistic and alternative therapies.], and his immediate reaction was to talk about studies that appear to show the existence of a neural network of some kind in the tissue of the heart – he described it as grey matter.

So it turns out that there is good evidence for all three cauldrons being the seat of some kind of intelligence, and as I began to weave this information together with my own experiences, I began to see the structure and pattern that, hopefully, I will share with you in this book.

The Cauldrons of Poesy

Translated by Erynn Rowan Laurie,
used with permission

Moí coire coir goiriath
gor rond n-ír Día dam a dúile dnemrib;
dliucht sóir sóerna broinn
bélrae mbil brúchtas úad.
Os mé Amargen glúngel garrglas gréliath,
gním mo goriath crothaib condelgib indethar
-- dath nád inonn airlethar Día do cach dóen,
de thoíb, ís toíb, úas toíb --
nemshós, lethshós, lánshós,
do h-Ébiur Dunn dénum do uath aidbsib ilib ollmarib;
i moth, i toth, i tráeth,
i n-arnin, i forsail, i ndínin-díshail,
sliucht as-indethar altmod mo choiri.

My perfect cauldron of warming
has been taken by the Gods from the mysterious abyss of the elements;
a perfect truth that ennobles from the center of being,
that pours forth a terrifying stream of speech.

I am Amirgen White-knee,
with pale substance and grey hair,
accomplishing my poetic incubation in proper forms,
in diverse colors.

The Gods do not give the same wisdom to everyone,
tipped, inverted, right-side-up;
no knowledge, half-knowledge, full knowledge --
for Eber Donn, the making of fearful poetry,
of vast, mighty draughts death-spells, of great chanting;
in active voice, in passive silence, in the neutral balance between,
in rhythm and form and rhyme,
in this way is spoken the path and function of my cauldrons.

Ciarm i tá bunadus ind airchetail i nduiniu; in i curp fa i n-anmain? As-berat araili bid i nanmain ar ní dénai in corp ní cen anmain. As-berat araili bid i curp in tan dano fo-glen oc cundu chorpthai .i. ó athair nó shenathair, ol shodain as fíru ara-thá bunad ind airchetail & int shois i cach duiniu chorpthu, acht cach la duine adtuíthi and; alailiu atuídi.

Where is the root of poetry in a person; in the body or in the soul? Some say it is in the soul, for the body does nothing without the soul. Some say it is in the body where the arts are learned, passed through the bodies of our ancestors. It is said that this is the truth remaining over the root of poetry, and the wisdom in every person's ancestry does not come from the northern sky into everyone, but into every other person.

Caite didiu bunad ind archetail & cach sois olchenae? Ní ansae; gainitir tri coiri i cach duiniu .i. coire goriath & coire érmai & coire sois.

What then is the root of poetry and every other wisdom? Not hard; three cauldrons are born in every person -- the cauldron of warming, the cauldron of motion and the cauldron of wisdom.

Coire goiriath, is é-side gainethar fóen i nduiniu fo chétóir. Is as fo dálter soas do doínib i n-ógoítu.

The cauldron of warming is born upright in people from the beginning. It distributes wisdom to people in their youth.

Coire érmai, immurgu, iarmo-bí impúd moigid; is é-side gainethar do thoib i nduiniu

The cauldron of motion, however, increases after turning; that is to say it is born tipped on its side, growing within.

Coire sois, is é-side gainethar fora béolu & is as fo-dáilter soes cach dáno olchenae cenmo-thá airchetal.

The cauldron of wisdom is born on its lips and distributes wisdom in poetry and every other art.

Coire érmai dano, cach la duine is fora béolu atá and .i. n-áes dois. Lethchlóen i n-áer bairdne & rand. Is fóen atá i n-ánshruithaib sofhis & airchetail. Conid airi didiu ní dénai cach óeneret, di h-ág is fora béolu atá coire érmai and coinid n-impoí brón nó fáilte.

The cauldron of motion then, in all artless people is on its lips. It is side-slanting in people of bardcraft and small poetic talent. It is upright in the greatest of poets, who are great streams of wisdom. Not every poet has it on its back, for the cauldron of motion must be turned by sorrow or joy.

Ceist, cis lir foldai fil forsin mbrón imid-suí? Ní ansae; a cethair: éolchaire, cumae & brón éoit & ailithre ar dia & is medón ata-tairberat inna cethair-se cíasu anechtair fo-fertar.

Question: How many divisions of sorrow turn the cauldrons of sages? Not hard; four: longing and grief, the sorrows of jealousy, and the discipline of pilgrimage to holy places. These four are endured internally, turning the cauldrons, although the cause is from outside.

Atáat dano dí fhodail for fíilte ó n-impoíther i coire sofhis, .i. fáilte déodea & fáilte dóendae.

There are two divisions of joy that turn the cauldron of wisdom; divine joy and human joy.

Ind fháilte dóendae, atáat cethéoir fodlai for suidi .i. luud éoit fuichechtae & fáilte sláne & nemimnedche, imbid bruit & biid co feca in duine for bairdni & fáilte fri dliged n-écse iarna dagfhrithgnum & fáilte fri tascor n-imbias do-fuaircet noí cuill cainmeso for Segais i sídaib, conda thochrathar méit motchnaí iar ndruimniu Bóinde frithroisc luaithiu euch aige i mmedón mís mithime dia secht mbliadnae beos.

There are four divisions of human joy among the wise – sexual intimacy, the joy of health and prosperity after the difficult years of studying poetry, the joy of wisdom after the harmonious creation of poems, and the joy of ecstasy from eating the fair nuts of the nine hazels of the Well of Segais in the Sidhe realm. They cast themselves in multitudes, like a ram's fleece upon the ridges of the Boyne, moving upstream swifter than racehorses driven on midsummer's day every seven years.

Fáilte déoldae, immurugu, tórumae ind raith déodai dochum in choiri érmai conid n-impoí fóen, conid de biit fáidi déodai & dóendai & tráchtairi raith & frithgnamo imale, conid íarum labrait inna labarthu raith & dogniat inna firthu, condat fásaige & bretha a mbríathar, condat desimrecht do cach cobrai. Acht is anechtair ata-tairberat inna hí-siu in coire cíasu medón fo-fertar.

The Gods touch people through divine and human joys so that they are able to speak prophetic poems and dispense wisdom and perform miracles, giving wise judgment with precedents, and blessings in answer to every wish. The source of these joys is outside the person and added to their cauldrons to cause them to turn, although the cause of the joy is internal.

> *ra-caun coire sofhis*
> *sernar dliged cach dáno*
> *dia moiget moín*
> *móras cach ceird coitchiunn*
> *con-utaing duine dán..*

> I sing of the cauldron of wisdom
> which bestows the nature of every art,
> through which treasure increases,
> which magnifies every artisan,
> which builds up a person through their gift.

> *Ar-caun coire n-érmai*
> *intlechtaib raith*
> *rethaib sofhis*
> *srethaib imbais*
> *indber n-ecnai*
> *ellach suíthi*
> *srúnaim n-ordan*
> *indocbáil dóer*
> *domnad insce*
> *intlecht ruirthech*
> *rómnae roiscni*
> *sáer comgni*
> *cóemad felmac*
> *fégthar ndliged*
> *deligter cíalla*
> *cengar sési*
> *sílaigther sofhis*
> *sonmigter soír*

sóerthar nád shóer,
ara-utgatar anmann
ad-fíadatar moltae
modaib dliged
deligthib grád
glanmesaib soíre
soinscib suad
srúamannaib suíthi,
sóernbrud i mberthar
bunad cach sofhis
sernar iar ndligiud
drengar iar frithgnum
fo-nglúaisi imbas
inme-soí fáilte
faillsigther tri brón;
búan bríg
nád díbdai dín.
Ar-caun coire n-érmai.

I sing of the cauldron of motion
understanding grace,
accumulating wisdom
streaming ecstasy as milk from the breast,
it is the tide-water of knowledge
union of sages
stream of splendor
glory of the lowly
mastery of speech
swift intelligence
reddening satire
craftsman of histories
cherishing pupils
looking after binding principles
distinguishing meanings
moving toward music
propagation of wisdom
enriching nobility
ennobling the commonplace
refreshing souls
relating praises
through the working of law

comparing of ranks
pure weighing of nobility
with fair words of the wise
with streams of sages,
the noble brew in which is boiled
the true root of all knowledge
which bestows according to harmonious principle
which is climbed after diligence
which ecstasy sets in motion
which joy turns
which is revealed through sorrow;
it is enduring fire
undiminished protection.
I sing of the cauldron of motion.

Coire érmai,
ernid ernair,
mrogaith mrogthair,
bíathaid bíadtair,
máraid márthair,
áilith áiltir,
ar-cain ar-canar,
fo-rig fo-regar,
con-serrn con-serrnar
fo-sernn fo-sernnar.

The cauldron of motion
bestows, is bestowed
extends, is extended
nourishes, is nourished
magnifies, is magnified
invokes, is invoked
sings, is sung
keeps, is kept,
arranges, is arranged,
supports, is supported.

Fó topar tomseo,
fó atrab n-insce,
fó comair coimseo
con-utaing firse.

Good is the well of poetry,
good is the dwelling of speech,
good is the union of power and mastery
which establishes strength.

Is mó cach ferunn,
is ferr cach orbu,
berid co h-ecnae,
echtraid fri borbu.

It is greater than every domain,
it is better than every inheritance,
it bears one to knowledge,
adventuring away from ignorance.

(Poem and interpretation can be found at
http://www.seanet.com/~inisglas/cauldronpoesy.html#poesytext)

Part One

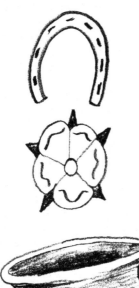

Exploring the Nature of Magick

Magick Defined

*M*agick is one of those words that can mean many different things, depending on the user. A stage conjurer sees magick as a skill of deception, consisting of sleight of hand and complex props designed to simulate something that should be impossible. To an anthropologist, magick is often seen as the primitive "explanation" for something that is not understood, or for scientific knowledge that is not in the public domain within a culture.

Even among modern western practitioners of the Occult arts, magick (with or without a "K") can mean one or more of a range of things. Aleister Crowley famously defined magick as "Magick is the science and art of causing Change to occur in conformity with Will", but even that lends itself to ambiguity.

Some practitioners see magick as nothing more than effective psychology, while others see it as the supernatural power - almost comic-book-worthy – we read about in folk tales and fairy stories, although most see it as something that falls between these two extremes, and partakes of both of them.

Personally, I believe in magick as something that can manifest real change in this world. From my own experience, I know that a well-constructed talisman can help someone get an assisted-living apartment in two weeks instead of the 18 months that the official told them it would take – I did that for my mother. I also know that proper focus and determination while chanting an ancient prayer to Osiris can turn back time – I did so in order to arrive at the end of a two-hour walk exactly ten minutes before I started that walk. My personal experiences with magick lead me to believe that some, if not all, of the techniques in the grimoires and spell-books can actually do what they say they can do. It just requires the application of the right techniques, the right state of mind, and the right keys to complete the puzzle.

One thing is certain – most spells and grimoires leave out key bits of information. They often describe the words and the actions, but leave out the mental or emotional component. These portions are reserved for the oral, face-to-face instruction from the adept who is your teacher. Of course that leads to an inevitable problem in the modern era – much of that oral teaching was never written down, and has died with the adepts who taught it. The Age of Reason, with its reliance on the new magick of Science has brought many benefits, and I believe that mostly this is a good thing. But by pushing religion and magick to the background, science has allowed vital information to die out, and then, when the magick no longer works, it justifies the demolition of lore and praxis by in effect saying "see, we told you it was all baloney!"

But what if we could rediscover those keys? What if we have actually had them with us all along, hidden in plain sight, and with a little effort we could restore them and start making the magick work again, the way it does in the myths, stories, legends and lore of our ancestors? It is my belief, based in part on the experiences that led me to write this book, that Visceral Magick is exactly that – the keys that are no longer taught because they are either forgotten, or not politically correct enough for our modern, safe society.

High vs. Low

When people talk about high and low magick, there are several ways to understand the term. For many people, the high/low split represents the difference between magick performed for mundane reasons (prosperity, jobs, healing, finding things, and so on) and performing magick that increases the magician's understanding of the cosmos (journeying between the realms, encountering deities and other spirits, working through the Mysteries in the form of various myths or stories). For others, the difference is between ceremonial magick of the kind taught by the Hermetic Order of the Golden Dawn, and the more shamanic magick of witches, crafters, and cunningfolk.

It will come as no surprise that, like so many things in Occult studies, both are essentially true. From the perspective of visceral magick, the first distinction is very real, but the visceral experiences help both kinds of magick equally, so there is no advantage to one form or another – besides the increased facility with magick that accompanies the spiritual evolution engendered by exploring the Mysteries.

But the second distinction is very important when working viscerally. Visceral magick, by its nature, is the diametric opposite of the intellectually oriented techniques of a High Magick lodge. Visceral magick engages the subconscious, the Visceral Intelligence, using the medium of the heart – emotions, feelings – to trigger and direct it. If the focus is all in the mind, it prevents the visceral intelligence from being involved, and so ceremonial magick techniques will not, on the whole, benefit from visceral experiences directly. There are, of course, exceptions, and an experienced ceremonialist may well be able to synthesize the two into a workable system. But this is not a task for the faint of heart.

Tools of the Trade

*I*t is often said that a true magician can work their magick stark naked in a concrete bunker, with no tools or regalia at all, and certainly an experienced practitioner should be able to work without anything but their own will. But that does not mean that the traditional "tools of the trade" are superfluous. First of all, these tools have value as training aids, in part because of what they symbolize, but primarily because they invoke a visceral reaction in the student as "things of power", and as such act as both training wheels and confidence boosters.

But it can truly be said that the tools of a traditional Crafter are perfectly selected to evoke a visceral response in both the practitioner and any observers, and that visceral response has a very real effect on the practitioner's ability to practice. They are, perhaps, the most accessible and obvious keys to visceral magick, and that gives them a very real, if indefinable, power in the manifest world.

The Cauldron

Cauldrons have been associated with magick ever since the alchemical act of cooking was discovered by our ancestors.

The Witch's Cauldron is a powerful symbol that represents many things – the Womb, the Tomb, mastery over herbs and potions, etc. For the practitioner who follows a Celtic path, it is also the Cauldron of Rebirth and the pearl-rimmed prototype of the Holy Grail, warmed by the breath of nine maidens.

As a Visceral Key or Trigger, the cauldron can be used in many ways. The symbolic value can be brought into play in ritual, where the cauldron's role as the Womb or the Tomb can evoke powerful emotional and visceral responses, or it can be used to contain the Bale Fire, or water for skrying as a group. There are many potent uses for the cauldron in a modern Crafter's rituals, but it comes into its own when it is placed at the center of the sacred space to act as the Well at the foot of the Bilé Tree. For as we gaze into the Well, we come to realize that we cannot tell if we are outside looking in, or inside looking out. This visceral combination of Sacred Well and Standing Tree, where the World Tree is truly turned topsy-turvy, brings one of the most potent paradoxes of the path to life, and once experienced, there is no turning back.

The Besom

It is rare to see a classic picture of a witch without her trusty broomstick. Old-style besoms, made of birch twigs, an ash shaft and willow bindings, are so much better for our purposes than the broomcorn brooms so often found in use in the neo-Pagan community. Once again, the classical symbolism is important, whether you subscribe to the "brush-forward" or "brush-backward" seating arrangement for flying on a broomstick. The besom is sometimes used for sweeping, but its primary use is for travelling between the worlds, whether that is by flying or by using it as a bridge to "cross the moat". Viscerally, it is both the boundary and the means to cross it, one of those paradoxes that crop up so often in magick, especially visceral magick.

The Skull

Bones in general – and skulls in particular – have always been part of the symbolism of magick, but it is in the hands of the visceral magician that the skull comes into its own. For crafters on the Crooked path, the skull represents the Ancestors, and sits upon the hearthstone to signify the central position of the

Ancestors in the tradition. But it is more than just a symbol – the skull is the gateway by which the Ancestors enter the sacred space when called, their focal point in the rituals. That this is a visceral trigger is never more apparent than the moment when the altar is activated and the Ancestors called at the start of every working. The celebrant calls on the Ancestors, then breathes life into the skull, literally blowing prana, or life-force, into it. The visceral experience is complete when the celebrant feels the skull become alive, when it blows back into their face.

The Stone

The hearthstone is the heart-stone, the central focal point of the coven. We blood the stone (place a drop of our blood on the hearthstone to seal an oath) when we make our oaths, it rests at the center of everything we do, and when we are claimed and acknowledged by the Ancestors as family, as fully-functioning master crafters within the tradition, they make a mark for each one of us upon the hearthstone. This is a moment of true visceral magick, as the crafter raises the Forge-Fire and summons the Ancestors – both acts of visceral magick and triggers in their own right – and is received by those Ancestors and acknowledged as family.

Because of this, the stone becomes a powerful focal point for Ancestral energy, and this adds to the seriousness with which oaths made upon it are held.

Traditions

*I*t is fairly safe to say that the word "tradition" is interpreted differently by every working group that uses it, as it is used to refer to themselves and define what they are and do. But in general terms, a tradition can be seen as a distinct magical path that is passed on by a combination of training and initiation at the hands of a qualified facilitator.

Within the overall universe of magical practice, there are a number of currents. These represent distinct flavors of magical lore and praxis, usually defined in cultural terms. For example, the Ancient Egyptian Mysteries are a current, within which you will find reconstructionist traditions, derived traditions, spiritual kin and eclectic traditions, all working with the myths and gods of Ancient Egypt with varying levels of adherence to the original practices that took place in the temples of Khem.

A current is the Great River of Blood, the sum of the wisdom, lore and experiences of the physical and spiritual ancestors who went before. Some of these currents, like the great rivers of the mundane world, divide into tributaries, or smaller rivers. These are the currents of groups, time periods or individual gods (or groups of gods) that exist as distinct entities within the greater cultural current. Our Egyptian example would include the currents of the Osirean Mysteries (Osiris, Isis and Horus), Sekhmet Mysteries (Sekhmet, Ptah and Imhotep), and Amun/Atum, as well as the time/place currents of Memphis, Thebes, and Heliopolis.

Within each of these currents we find the Traditions, or Schools, of specific paths of magick. Continuing our example, we have the Followers of Horus (Pert em Hru), the Four Orders, and in modern times the Fellowship of Isis, the Kemetic Orthodox Church, and the Hermetic Brotherhood of Luxor, among many other traditions. While they will undoubtedly share elements of lore and practical technique with other traditions, they will almost certainly have their own specific body of ritual practices, versions of myths, and philosophical discourse or wisdom material.

My personal definition of a tradition requires three generations of practitioners – there needs to be the founder or founders, plus their students, and their students' students, for it to be a tradition. Otherwise, while it may be a valid and powerful component of the current, it is more correctly described as a path.

Many people place a great deal of importance on the lineage aspects of a tradition. Who you were initiated by, and who they were initiated by, often appears to be more important than what you know or what you do. From a visceral perspective, this is much less important... your lineage defines a lot about your practice, but it is your intuitive grasp of the material and your personal experience with it that matters most, as that is what brings the magick of your path, tradition or current to manifestation.

Folklore

Folklore is a rich source for modern crafters. It contains many snippets of lore, both philosophical and practical, and many of the stories are good triggers for visceral experiences. Some even describe visceral experiences, such as the tales of visits to Elphame.

Much like poetry, folk tales are best experienced by listening to a good storyteller. There is something magical in the way hearing the stories and poems engage the imagination, that is quite different from the way reading them does. It is as if the storyteller adds a little visceral magick of their own, which brings the stories to life.

One of the ways that the stories of our Gods and ancestors can be of value is as repositories of practical or philosophical wisdom. A great example of this is the story of Gwion Bach, which is a wonderful allegory for the process of initiation into the Mysteries. But while the metaphors and imagery contained within it are – quite literally – food for thought, those images, and the carefully crafted sequence of events described in the story combine with the emotional intensity provided by the story's pace in conjunction with the crafting of a good story by the storyteller to evoke a powerful emotional and visceral response in the heart of the listener. This is why ancient sages would say of stories like this, that hearing them regularly could lead to enlightenment without any further work.

Essentially, a well-crafted story created by a skilled esotericist not only evokes the strong emotions that produces the visceral reaction, but transforms and channels the energy thus raised in specific ways, designed to bring about the desired outcome. In the case of the story of Gwion Bach, the aim is to enable the listener to follow in the footsteps of Gwion/Taliesin and achieve that inner initiation facilitated by union with godhead. And in the course of doing so, the heart cauldron is set upright to fill with the creative energy that enables the student to reach their potential.

Working with the Cauldrons

*T*he Cauldrons of Poesy are a useful framework on which to hang the mechanics of visceral magick, and while I have no proof of this, I suspect that our Celtic ancestors may well have used them in a similar fashion.

We will look at each cauldron in turn, but here are the points that apply to all three cauldrons:

1. The language of the Gods is poetry, as demonstrated in "The White Goddess", by Robert Graves. More precisely, the key to working directly with the visceral intellect is poetic thought, so it is important to make poetry a part of your daily life. Ideally, poetry should be listened to, so if you do have to read it alone, read it out loud, so you are still listening to it. To complete the effect of poetry in your life, you should be composing your own poetry too.

2. The key to awakening your visceral awareness is visceral experiences. These are triggered by techniques, by lore, and by powerful emotions. Try to expose yourself to one or more of these triggers daily.

3. The key to maximizing the effect of the experiences is to surrender to them. Do not try to analyze them until after the experience is done, or you will cut them short as the cerebral intellect takes over.

If you follow these three points, and incorporate them into your daily life, you will find that your magical and mundane lives will become more integrated, until they are one and the same. Along the way, you will develop the ability to control the magick so that it does not distract you from necessary mundane concerns, but it is there the moment you need to call on it.

Because you have a guide and an outline of what to do, you should find that you will get results quite quickly, as long as you enter into it wholeheartedly. I was stumbling along in the dark, figuring it all out as I went, and from my first noticing the effect to full integration took about two years. With a plan and a passion, you should be able to reach that point in a year, and the results should continue growing as long as you are working the system.

The aim of this work is to "tip" the cauldrons into upright positions, the first cauldron being initially inverted and then uprighted. It is not easy to explain in words exactly what this means, as it is partially a metaphor, yet wholly a real thing. By tipping the cauldrons, we mean that the energy centers, or power points, or whatever you feel they are, become optimized, in the same way that exercises to open the chakras will optimize their effectiveness. In this case, it is not necessary to meditate or visualize the cauldrons tipping – just be aware of them and let the experiences and emotions do the rest.

Most of your efforts will be in the area of the second cauldron, the Cauldron of Motion, as this is essentially the only one that you can affect directly and consciously. For the longest time I was convinced that the first cauldron had to be tipped before you would get any tangible results, but I have realized recently that this is not a linear process. Essentially, your efforts should focus upon righting the second cauldron, using the powerful emotional responses and visceral experiences to make sure that you can maximize your potential. Then at some point you will trigger a deep Underworld experience that will tip the Cauldron of Warming into the Underworld, collecting energy and establishing a permanent link. This is an initiatory experience that can take many forms, but is often referred to as "awakening the Dragon".

Once you have engaged the lower cauldron, the Cauldron of Warming, you will find that your progress picks up pace exponentially, and that your potential is expanded. More importantly, this is the point, in my experience, where your magick becomes integrated with your mundane life, and is manifest to the point where you feel magical energy as a physical force in your life: your body responding to it with the same responses you get from static electricity and physical winds – hair standing on end, goose bumps, and feeling it as a "physical" force.

Then the real fun begins. It is as if you have expanded the capacity of the Cauldron of Warming, so your potential is greater, leading you to do greater things and have stronger, more potent visceral experiences. Whatever tradition you follow, you will find that this stage empowers the praxis of your path, leading to greater and more frequent success from your crafting, and essentially more power in your magick.

Now you are working to refine the process. First of all, you strive to make the second cauldron, the Cauldron of Motion, stable in the upright position – at first it is prone to tip back on its side, or even turn upside down (in other words, the change in state is not stable), as the experiences and emotions continue to affect the movement of the cauldron. But as you continue to work on it, the cauldron will eventually settle in the chosen position and become stable, at which point you will find that your magick has become reliable, and it is likely that you will also find that any creative talents you may have will be more consistent and improved.

Once the second cauldron is stable – not everyone will get to this stage – your training, whether formal or "self-study" will become the focus of your efforts, as you seek to bring about the conditions that will turn the third and final cauldron, the Cauldron of Wisdom, into the upright position. The poem states that this can be done through proper training or by divine intercession, but I suspect it requires a little of both. When the Cauldron of Wisdom is upright, it acts as a kind of "satellite dish" to the Gods, and permits the practice of Imbas, or "poetic frenzy" to occur. Traditionally, this involves speaking about the Gods or speaking as one of the Gods, in a most eloquent and poetic manner, but I suspect that this is more because the poem speaks in terms of becoming a bard, than because of any real limitation there. It is my belief that this is just one example of the type of divine gift that may be expressed, and that each person will find it expressed as an amplification and evolution of the gift or gifts they already possess.

It is unlikely, and in my opinion undesirable, that the Cauldron of Wisdom will remain in a stable upright position. Rather, I believe that it will turn upright when needed, and remain inverted at other times. This will enable the adept to retain their sanity and interact fairly normally with the rest of society, as the orientation of this cauldron will of necessity dictate where your focus lies... on the Cosmos and the Gods, or inward to your own life and vitality. To be permanently "between the worlds" is not practical outside of a monastery.

Part Two

The Cauldron of Warming

Initiation and Initiatory Experiences

Contrary to popular belief, initiation is not the goal of studying magick - it is the beginning point. The word comes from the Latin "inire", to go into, enter upon, or begin. Anything that comes before is a process of finding the path, checking to see if it is a good path to try, and then finding the gateway to enter onto the path proper. It is only after the point of initiation that the student truly begins to learn anything more than generic, public domain material. This is the traditional perspective, and while I would not hesitate to say that it is not rigid and without exception, on the whole I would say it matches the way things work, based on my own experience and observation.

Of course, that then raises the question about where initiation comes from. This depends on which of several aspects of initiation we are talking about, because there is more than one kind of initiation. Let's start with the simplest.

Initiation into a tradition and/or a working group is a rite of passage. It is a formal recognition that the candidate is becoming "one of us", and is bestowed by the group, or the group's leader. This kind of initiation usually involves some kind of test of worthiness, that may or may not be a formality, followed by an oath or promise, and the presentation of regalia or the making of marks upon the body that denote the candidate's new status as a member of the tribe.

Initiation into the Mysteries is something else entirely, though it may coincide with the rite of passage. This initiation comes from within, from your ancestors and gods, though it can be facilitated by a skillful mentor. It involves a very real test, usually in the form of some kind of personal sacrifice, often depicted as the candidate being "broken open" or "cracked" to free the spirit within. This is often accomplished by an underworld encounter with a Chthonic initiator, terrifying in form to the candidate, and is often followed by a rebirth of some kind into a new state of being.

In many modern groups, initiation occurs as a kind of ritual theater, where the actual process is symbolized by an enactment of a Legend involving heroes or deities specific to the tradition. In too many cases, the theatrical aspect is stressed rather than the visceral aspect, and the rites become a formality along the lines of initiation into the Freemasons or college fraternities. That is not to say that the rites don't have power, they do. But without a facilitator who understands the need to raise them above the level of a theatrical performance, their effect is purely at the psychological level, as a rite of passage, and any real internal initiation is left to occur by itself.

That said, it is not uncommon for that inner initiation to take place in the days or weeks following the formal one. But with a skilled facilitator at the helm, and an understanding of when the candidate is truly ripe to be "plucked from the bough", the two can be brought together in a powerful ceremony that affects the candidate - and the other participants - at every level of their being. This is the essence of visceral magick, and gives the student the greatest chance of developing their own visceral connections. The price that is paid by the groups that do this, is that there is a very real possibility that the candidate will fail(a very traumatic experience for all concerned). Without that danger, it is very difficult to create the intensity needed to get everyone to the right point. Depending on where and how the candidate fails, it may be possible to try again after a period of reflection and more training, but frequently the failure is the end of that particular path for the student.

In tribal cultures, there is a recognition that somebody may be prepared for an initiation, or may come upon one spontaneously, because the triggers that are deliberately applied can also occur by chance. Extreme illness or near-death experiences are rarely used deliberately, but they are as effective at bringing someone to the threshold of initiation as the carefully managed techniques of the teacher, and just like the deliberate techniques, the outcome depends solely on what the student does next. Either way, the experiences are extremely visceral, and among other things open the student up to the reality of the worlds beyond this one.

Instant Visceral Triggers

Visceral triggers can be bundled into three types: the ones that are purely mechanical and result in an instant visceral experience; the ones that take you to a place or state where you may have visceral experiences if you are ready for them; and the ones that plant seeds in your psyche that later germinate into dreams or other altered state experiences that themselves trigger visceral interactions. Obviously in the beginning the instant visceral triggers are the most useful, though a dedicated teacher, if you have one, will be laying the groundwork for the other kinds of visceral experience from day one. For the solo practitioner, the instant triggers are indispensible.

Sensory Deprivation

In the noisy hubbub of modern urban life, it is rare for us to be free of background noise, and so people came up with the sensory deprivation chamber. This consists of a tank or bath filled with salt water at body temperature, where the subject lies floating in the darkness, with no sound breaking in. The idea is that for the average person, after between 3 and 4 hours, the mind gets so bored that it begins to create visual and aditory hallucinations, and the subject becomes fully immersed in a waking dream. The experience can be enhanced and sped up with the judicious use of trance or drugs, though research on this has fallen out of favor. It is also an expensive set-up.

There are cheaper ways of doing this, though, especially for someone who has learnt to enter trance states. A reclining chair or a bed is the only real expense, but most people have one or both of these already. A good blindfold, or heavy curtains that will enable the room to be totally dark, will take care of visual stimulation, and a radio tuned between stations, where there is only white noise, will effectively eliminate noises from outside the room. Interestingly, research has shown that exposure to white noise for 4-6 hours will often cause the subject to hallucinate, all by itself.

The subject sits in the chair or lies on the bed in total darkness, and listens to the white noise. Entering into a trance-state, they get to the "floaty" stage, where they have effectively cancelled out the input from their mundane senses, allowing them to focus on their higher senses.

Sensory Overload

The opposite of sensory deprivation is sensory overload, and this is the method that was used classically, in the form of a Witches' cradle or suspension from hooks through the skin. Generally seen as a risky exercise in modern times, these classical techniques have fallen out of favor with magical practitioners, though they have been taken up enthusiastically by various other subcultures. They are expensive to set up safely, and there are definitely issues about trust and the potential for litigation to take into account. Luckily, there are cheaper and safer methods that are just as authentic, and more importantly, just as effective.

These other methods can be as simple as spinning someone around, especially while blindfolded, pushing them around a circle of people while making a cacophony of noise, but perhaps the favorite method is ecstatic dance. This is a technique that has been embraced by many cultures, including some branches of Christianity. Wild, uninhibited dance movements are combined with powerful rhythms on drums, and it doesn't take long for the dancers to be deeply entranced. The trick here is to then harness all that and direct it in a spiritual, magical direction. This is exactly what we see in the Voodoo ceremonies in New

Orleans, and in the tribal dances of Australian Aboriginals, Amazon hunters and African tribes, to name just a few.

The Scourge

Many traditional crafters tend to look down on Wicca as the "light" form of witchcraft. But as it was practiced during Gardner's day, there is nothing "fluffy" about real Wicca.

For Gardner, the trance-inducing tool of choice was the scourge. Many have criticized him as a "dirty old man" bringing his BDSM into his rites, but to tell the truth, the Scourge Ritual has almost no BDSM elements, as the aim is blood control, not pain/pleasure.

Combined with the restriction of blood-flow provided by the accompanying cords, the carefully applied ministrations of the scourge help to draw blood away from the brain, causing a deep trance state that combines with the deliberately hypnotic movements of the scourger and the highly charged symbolism and energy of the ritual itself to free the spirit from the intellect and physical form. The subject flies free, able to travel between the worlds, and after the rite is over, having had the proverbial veil lifted, is able to make good use of the subtle senses and trigger more visceral encounters.

The scourge ritual found in the Gardnerian Book of Shadows is an effective way of using the scourge to invoke a visceral experience, though I have personally introduced a few tweaks here and there to enhance it in that direction. Firstly, it is important to remember that, whatever the symbolism of the cords, they are actually there to restrict blood-flow, so care should be taken in exactly where to put them and how tight to tie them. In my personal practice, I place the "knee" cord higher on the thigh, in order to better restrict the flow. This is a higher-risk location, so it is important for facilitator and subject to communicate as the cords are being tied, to ensure they are neither too tight nor too loose.

With the subject bound and lying across a stool or other seat of appropriate height - I find piano stools are perfect for this - the facilitator stands in front of them, and scourges with a regular rhythm, targeting the lower back with slightly exaggerated strokes, so that the regular rhythmic movement seen in the periphery of the subject's vision adds to the hypnotic, trance-inducing effect. As with tying the cords, there should be communication between the subject and facilitator at the start, to make sure that the scourge strokes are neither too hard nor too soft. You do not want to be causing actual pain, but the strokes should be firm enough to redden the skin. The stroke should connect low on the subject's back, then the scourge should be drawn up the back towards the facilitator as it is returned for the next stroke. This results in the stroke being followed by a light, stroking caress that stimulates the flesh of the back in between hits, adding a complex counterpoint to the regular rhythm and adding to the trance-inducing effect.

This careful application of the scourge makes use of hypnotic rhythms as well as further drawing the blood away from the brain by reddening the skin, and a trance is established quite quickly. Traditionally forty strokes are given as the "perfect sacrifice", and in the Wiccan initiation this number is comprised of smaller subsets of significant numbers, but for our purposes this is only a guideline. The facilitator should continue the scourge strokes until they perceive that the subject has entered a significant trance-state.

Sex as a Trigger
(Orgasm, and Eroto-Comatose Lucidity)

Pagans these days seem to either embrace sex at every opportunity, or shun it completely. But there is no escaping the simple fact that for all practical purposes, sexual energy and magical energy are essentially the same. Therefore raising sexual energy is a quick and effective way or raising magical energy, and it comes as no surprise, therefore, that sex and sex-play, and even simple sexual tension, can evoke visceral experiences.

The simplest example is the consecration of cake and ale in Wicca, also known as the symbolic Great Rite. Wiccans tend to do this with a chalice and athame, or dagger, but I prefer the more overt symbolism of the chalice and wand. For those not familiar with the process, the wine or ale in the chalice is consecrated by simulating the union of the God and Goddess by plunging the blade or wand into the chalice. Most Wiccans do this very formally, using words such as "as the athame is to the male, so the chalice is to the female, and when brought forth together, they invoke beauty, joy, and that expression of true happiness, which is perfect love." Some Wiccans do engage in a measure of sauciness in the process of doing this, but on the whole it is played as straight as the equivalent part of the Catholic Mass.

Personally, I believe that, when done correctly, there is no such thing as a symbolic Great Rite. In other words, if you do it right, it is an act of supreme consummation that transcends the actual method of expression. Using the chalice and wand are no different from using female and male genitalia, because what starts as a symbolic act is made real by the energy and visceral participation of the performers.

I have had many occasions to demonstrate this in my Visceral Magick workshops, where I have partnered my own coveners, friends, strangers, and even on one occasion another man, and everyone has felt the sexual tension, the release, and the true magick of the technique. When done correctly, it is not only the couple performing the consecration that get swept up in the climax of the experience, but all who are present in the rite. The best way to describe this is a whole body orgasm that somehow does not have a physical component - a grand shiver that flows through the entire body.

Needless to say, an actual physical orgasm can also be used as a visceral trigger, and this is - or was before everyone became prudes - a powerful way of raising energy and manifesting the desired outcome of a spell. At its most simple level, an individual, couple or group, focus on a particular outcome while engaging in sexual stimulation, and at the point of orgasm each person throws their energy, intent, and the orgasmic energy into a visualization of the desired result. Obviously it is not easy to focus so well at the point of orgasm, it takes training and practice. But this can be augmented by having a visual representation, a painting, photograph or sigil to focus on, and one experienced practitioner can be required to gather and focus the energies, allowing less experienced partners to participate, and gain experience.

Eroto-comatose lucidity is a technique favored by A. O. Spare and Aleister Crowley. It involves bringing the subject to orgasm multiple times, until they fall into an exhausted trance. It can be conducted by multiple complete orgasms, or by repeatedly bringing the subject to the point of orgasm and then falling back, denying the orgasm, for up to a dozen times. The resulting orgasm that is released on the final time is mind-blowingly powerful, and leaves the subject in a deep trance well-suited for oracular work. This technique can be done by a couple, or a group of facilitators working on a single subject, but it is important for all concerned to be disciplined and not let the ritual just become sex.

Descent into the Wasteland

The triggers described so far are great for experiencing a taste of visceral magick, but in order for it to become a living part of your magical practice, you need to tip the Cauldron of Warming over long enough to connect with the Underworld and establish an initiatory and energetic link with it. One of the simplest ways of doing this is to undertake the experience of the Descent into the Wasteland.

The Wasteland is a location or state of existence taken from the Arthurian tales. In the stories, the Wasteland is ruled by the Fisher King, who has been wounded in the thigh - a medieval euphemism for being emasculated. In other words, he is incomplete and without his power, and consequently the land he rules is laid to waste. In the story, the arrival of the Holy Grail heals him, and restores the Land, and in many ways this visceral experience does the same for us, because our modern mundane lives have been carefully designed to cut us off from our "flights of fancy", the potency we get from connecting to the darkness at the heart of our being, the Underworld (which exists both within us and separate from us as the Underworld "plane").

The following exercise may need to be performed several times before it "takes" - in a group, the ones who went before lend their experience to the exercise, ensuring that the person undertaking it for the first time makes it at least as far as encountering the true wasteland. But the solo practitioner needs to build up a momentum to carry them to the heart of the wasteland, and then keep them there long enough to fulfil their task.

Start by triggering a viscerally receptive state with one of the triggers above. Essentially any effective trance inducer will work. Once you have done that, it is time to take the Widdershins Walk, or Treading the Mill.

Heading counter-clockwise, or widdershins, begin to tread the mill. You should be moving with a shambling gait, arms swaying from side to side, with your back bent and your head down. This helps you to really feel the grinding down of the "millstone" that really assists in the process. As you go round, imagine yourself descending down the inner wall of a vast cauldron or well. The deeper you go, the more resistance there is, and the greater the weight on your back becomes.

At some point, you will feel that you have gone far enough, and you will feel a weight on your back, literally "the Devil on your back." At this point you turn into the center of the working space, the center of the Mill you have been treading, and begin to reach in to the cold black core that you sense in the center of your being. As you do so, you realize that by descending, you have taken your place as king of this place, and that the cold black core at your own heart is, in fact, the black interior sun at the center of the earth, the hearth of the group, and your own coal-black heart.

Let the pressure build - you will feel like a head of steam is building up, until it cracks the fragile shell of you underworld body, leaving only a brilliant golden-white light, exploding forth with a scream. At this point you drop to the floor, and just let it all go - primal scream, total release. The "devil on your back" is the baggage you carry with you daily, and this exercise will release you from that. The trick here is that the "beast" you release in the Wasteland immediately sees and is seen by your own higher self, and it is this spark of angel and devil that creates the heat to fuse everything together. Allowing yourself to rise up out of nothingness, your ascent causes the cauldron to right itself once more, containing within it the fire from the interior sun. Then you are ready to use this energy to work on the second cauldron.

Techniques to Trigger Visceral Experiences

aside from the descent into the Wasteland, there are other techniques found in various cultures that can be used to turn the Cauldron of warming and make the necessary Underworld initiatory connection. They are frequently encountered in the tribal cultures that can be found in remote areas of the world, but also in the folk tales of Britain, Europe, and even some areas of the United States.

Near-Death and Sickness

Many tribal shamans and witchdoctors start their career with a near-death experience or life-threatening illness. Most of these are the kind of illness or injury that causes coma-inducing fevers, where nothing can be done for the patient except keep them comfortable, try to cool the fever, and hope that it breaks before their body does. Interestingly, while this is obviously a rather extreme "rite of passage" it strongly resembled the deliberately induced vision quests of antiquity, from the Druidic vigil atop Cader Idris or wrapped in the traditional white bull's hide (which, while a literal tool of initiation for our ancestors, could well be a metaphor for the classical Body of Light), to the three nights in the sarcophagus of the Ancient Egyptian pyramid initiation (described in Many P. Hall's "Secret Teachings of All Ages", and by various Greek scholars). It seems that many cultures make use of the vision quest, but if the technology or skill is not present to induce it deliberately, they take advantage of times when it occurs naturally.

Dark Night of the Soul

The Dark Night of the Soul can be expressed in a number of different cultural experiences, but just like the vision quest or near-death experience, they all appear to have several points in common.

The Dark Night of the Soul refers to an experience that is said to immediately precede initiation, when the candidate's own shadow self comes to mock them and challenge them. This can take the form of the doppelganger that confronts you with every bad or negative thing that you have done, or merely presents you with a record of your life, leaving you to judge yourself. Or it can be in the form of the Devil you wrestle in order to win the prize - that wrestling can be literal, in the form of a challenge of some sort, or an interplay of words. In the southern US, there is the "dark stranger at the crossroads", often assumed to be the Devil, who trades a shill or gift for the soul of the one waiting there, while in the UK, it is the White Goddess or the Lord of the Mound (the traditional Crossroads God, also known as Death or the Devil in some areas) who meets you under the gibbet, riding on a goat.

Other versions may involve preparing a charm, such as the Toad Bone, which you then have to keep hold of in the graveyard, while the Devil tries to take it from you. They all involve a barter, a contest, or an exchange of some kind, but the person who prevails comes away with a gift of great value, usually in the form of a gift, not always supernatural... In the southern US there are many tales of people who waited at the crossroads to barter their soul for virtuosity at playing the guitar, or the piano, or the gift of oration.

By listening to these tales, we embed their essence in our being, which can lead to dreams or even waking experiences that fall into this category - though waiting at the crossroads should always be a conscious choice, it can certainly be enhanced by listening to the stories of those who came before.

Tearing Down and Building Up

Rites of passage often involve a component where the candidate is, metaphorically speaking, ripped apart and then put back together again. The general idea is that the candidate must be remade in the image of their new "family", but in order to do that, all the old identifiers are removed. All over the planet you will find these experiences.

As an underworld initiation, many European countries have tales of descending into a subterranean blacksmith's shop. The candidate is taken apart, bone by bone, and the dismembered bones are boiled up. Finally, the candidate is given new bones, often of gold or silver, and is rebuilt with various talismans, sigils and other magical things, hidden by the new golden flesh, implying both strength and authority added to the candidate's original qualities.

Encountering Fairies

There are many tales of encountering Faeries (whichever spelling of the word is used), or the Road to Elphame, as these encounters are often called. Many tales tell of a traveler who follows a stag or some other creature, or a fair maiden, through a gap in a hedge, or between two standing stones, to find themselves in the Faery Kingdom, where they are treated hospitably through an evening of merry-making, to wake next morning back in our world, only to find months or years have passed.

Listening to these tales being told will prime your dreams for experiences of your own, and maybe waking experiences as well. I have had the good fortune to see a white stag running through the forest in Ashridge, while collecting holly etc. for Yule. My great regret is that I did not pursue it.

Pilgrimage to Sacred Sites

Never underestimate the potential of visits to sacred sites. Many of these places have tales attached to them that are ideal for promoting visceral experiences. A tale told next to the actual site where all or part of the story actually happened can be exponentially more powerful than the same story told at home. Some sites are so magical that they don't even need their story to be told.

Quite a few years ago, I was visiting Glastonbury for the very first time, with my brother. On our first day in town, after we arrived and got settled in our hotel, we decided we couldn't wait, and decided to go and visit Glastonbury Tor. As it was foggy and dull, with a steady drizzle of light rain, our wives decided to stay at the hotel and sample their selection of ciders, while my brother and I set off for the Tor.

Because the weather was fairly unpleasant, we had the whole place to ourselves. The walk up the hill was accomplished without seeing another person, and we started to feel that something special was happening, especially when we saw a hawk swoop down out of the sky and catch a snake, flying off with the serpent caught tight in its claws. We looked at each other, then continued the final part of the climb, soon reaching the tower at the top.

As we approached the tower, I thought there was something wrong with my eyes, because as I looked through the arch at the base of the tower, I could see a bright, sun-lit sky, despite the fact that the sky all around was grey and damp. I asked my brother if he could see it, and he told me that he could. We both felt an overwhelming urge to walk through it, but mindful of the stories about such things, and even more mindful of how our wives would react if we disappeared for a month or two, we elected to choose discretion over valor, and stayed in the realm of mankind.

There are many sacred sites that are, according to local legends, portals to other realms, usually at specific times of the year. Whether it is a cairn or burial mound, or a place that is natural yet otherworldly, such as Alderney Edge, the legends associated with these places are ripe with lore that we can allow to permeate the visceral intellect in order to experience something special at these sacred places.

Taking Alderney Edge as an example, it is a red sandstone escarpment overlooking the village of Alderney, and along with it most of the county of Cheshire. There have been settlements in the area since the Bronze Age, and it is a site of copper mining. Some magnificent legends have grown around the area, including the one about the iron gates. These mysterious gates are said to be located between Stormy Point and the Holy Well, though nobody is sure exactly where they are.

The story is that a farmer was taking a white horse to sell at market, when an old man in flowing grey robes stopped him and offered to buy the horse. As the sum offered was less than he thought the horse was worth, the farmer refused. The old man said he would be at the same spot that evening, when the farmer returned home having failed to sell the horse. Sure enough, the horse was not sold, and on the way home the old man appeared and offered to buy the horse for the same amount. This time the farmer agreed to sell it, at which point the old man banged his staff on the ground and the rock of the escarpment rolled back to reveal a set of iron gates. The old man opened the gates, and asked the farmer to bring the horse inside, into a large cavern.

Inside the cavern, the farmer saw countless men and horses, all fast asleep. The old man told him that they were warriors, waiting for a time when England was in danger, at which point they would awaken to fight in defense of the Land. People have speculated over the years that the old man was Merlin, and the knights were Arthur's army, waiting to heed his call to battle once more.

So the trick is to visit sites that have a history and mythology that relates to - or at least resonates with - your tradition and your ancestry. By allowing the lore and myths to come to life within you, you will learn much about the Mysteries, and strengthen your visceral magick.

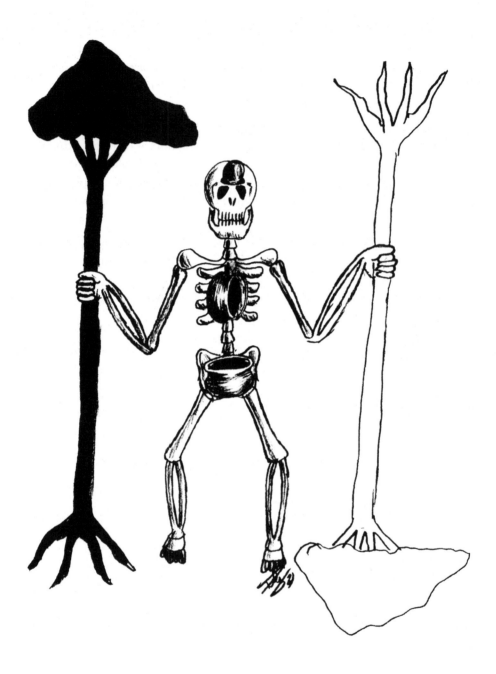

Visceral Experiences

This kind of visceral experience is much easier to do on purpose, though it can still happen spontaneously, and a little planning can really help you get the most out of your work. Even if you do not have a place you can get to that has the required lore, history and connection to your ancestors, it is possible to build such a place from scratch. Here is an account of an actual visceral encounter I had, followed by some ideas on how to create your own sacred spaces.

Encountering Herne in Windsor Royal Park

Many years ago I earned a living by singing and playing my guitar. On this particular occasion, I was singing and playing as part of a duo, and we had a Christmas Eve gig in an Italian restaurant in London. My wife was pregnant, which was seen as very good luck by the family that owned the restaurant, and they insisted that we sit down to dinner with them after the gig - which, considering the date, meant we were eating with the family well after midnight.

So it was that we found ourselves driving home in a pre-dawn fog, and we got completely lost. We realized this when we were finally able to see the sides of the road, and noticed we were driving through parkland. As it began to get lighter, a great tree loomed out of the fog, and we decided to pull over and try to get our bearings.

I got out of the car, and wandered toward the tree, beginning to realize that we had somehow ended up driving through Windsor Royal Park. The tree we stopped by looked impressive enough to be the Great Royal Oak I had read about, and just as I was thinking this to myself, I heard the sounds of hooves and baying hounds, and turned around to see a hunt emerging from the mist. Horses, hounds, and people, vaguely noticed on the backs of the horses, I thought it was the local fox hunt, until I saw the great steed bearing the Master of the Hunt. The power and potency in his bearing was unmistakable... neither were the magnificent antlers reaching out on either side of his brow. I found myself staring up at Herne Himself, as he paused, nodded to me, then spurred his horse past me and the tree, and on off into the mist again. As the hoof beats and howls faded away, I stood there, speechless, feeling truly blessed to have experienced this piece of lore. It was a simple thing, but it affected me deeply.

Creating New Sacred Sites

So, what can you do if you cannot travel to the sacred sites of your ancestors? Obviously for a crafter in the US, while it is possible to travel to Europe to visit these sites, the cost necessitates that it is a rare treat rather than a regular thing. But as I learnt in my experiment about calling the Land and the Ancestors from various cities around the world, the Sacred Landscape is with us wherever we go, lying under the cover of the local culture - you just need to dig a little deeper than in the "homeland".

There are certain types of sacred site that lend themselves to being created here and now, and they are cairns, standing stones, wells and caves. The first three can be built, and the last can be found; then it is simply a matter of sanctifying them and then "powering them up" by working with them through a cycle of the Wheel of the Year.

A cairn can be a simple pile of rocks, or it can be the trilithon that would be found inside a burial mound. Both versions act as a kind of memorial, and so lend themselves to Ancestral workings. One idea is to make either kind of cairn as an outdoor altar, and when working outside, place your hearthstone, if you use one, upon it. For a cairn, a simple dedication to one or more specific ancestors, followed by working seasonal rites on it for a full year (as stated above), will lay a good foundation.

Standing stones can be approached in several ways. Firstly, a single standing stone can be set up in a way that is significant to a particular deity or ancestor. You could set up a large gold-capped stone for Cromh, for example, with four smaller stones set about it to carry lanterns or candles. We actually do this in miniature in our temple. Or for Llew, for example, you can set up a facsimile of the stone on the bank of the Cynfal river in Wales, with its hole pierced by the spear Llew threw at Gronw. In this case we might make a stone look like the original, which still stands by the river, complete with the hole, and place it by a stream or pond. Then, we would work rituals built upon the story of Llew and Blodeuwedd (from the Mabinogion) through the course of the year, culminating in the spear-throw of Llew.

Caves and other natural sites might lend themselves to a retelling of the stories of your Gods or Ancestors, in which case you just need to work out a cycle of rites to work in the location chosen. All of these require the spirit of the Land to be invoked, so that it might recognize and bond with the mythos being created, resulting in modern sacred sites that are as potent as some of the ancient sites, especially where awakening the visceral intellect is concerned.

Part Three

The Cauldron of Movement

Intense Emotions and Fulfilling your Potential

*I*t is said that in order to fulfil your potential, the Cauldron of Movement must be set upright. The idea is that a cauldron on its side can still hold some liquid, because of its spherical nature, but it is only when it is upright that it can be filled to the brim. The Cauldrons of Poesy poem refers specifically to Bardic ability, but in actuality, the potential we are talking about here is not limited to composing poems or singing. Any and all magical and creative abilities come under the influence of the Cauldron of Movement, and it is our overall ability that is affected by how full our cauldron is.

So it is important to turn the cauldron upright, which we do by making use of powerful emotions. It is important to remember two things during this process. The first is that it does not matter whether the emotions are positive or negative – they can all be used to turn the cauldron. The second thing is that the cauldron does not become fixed in place once it is upright. Intense emotions will also turn it back on its side from the upright position. For this reason, it is best to work on turning it upright via a visceral experience before any magical or creative endeavor, until it finally settles in that position predominantly.

Essentially, it appears that over time the turning becomes easier, until you reach a point where upright is its normal resting position... I think it is how full the cauldron is that dictates this – a full cauldron is more stable than an empty one, and so it more easily stays in the position you left it in.

Instant Visceral Triggers

*I*nstant Visceral Triggers are very useful tools for ritual work, because they induce a trance-state and open everyone up to visceral awareness directly. This is especially useful if you have a mix of experienced and "newbie" ritualists participating in the rite, as it brings everyone to approximately the same "space" quickly and efficiently. Obviously some techniques lend themselves to specific types of ritual, but there are plenty to choose from, and some will work admirably for most situations.

Agony and Ecstasy

Pain and pleasure provoke strong emotional responses, which in turn create the kind of energy that can turn the cauldron. It is for this reason that they have historically been used in rituals for millennia. Of course, the pain and pleasure can be literal, or they can also be metaphorical, and this can be seen in politics as well – the emotions engendered by Hitler's Nuremberg Rally speeches caught the crowd into a hateful fervor, and entranced by his rhythmic, passionate delivery, the crowd offered up control of their group mind to him, enabling him to "ride the dragon" and use their power for his own evil ends.

On a smaller, more ethical scale, the skilled visceral magician can "fan the flames" of passion in the other ritualists, using poetry, prose, physical pain or pleasure to create and maintain those powerful emotions. This can also be done through ritual theater, and I believe that was its original purpose. But in modern times the emphasis has shifted from this to focus on the drama and the theater, attempting to re-enact a story rather than use it to create a passionate response.

Physical pleasure and pain, in the form of sadomasochistic play, is a more specialized field, though elements of this can be found in classic ritual forms. Whether it is a touch of kinkiness or carefully prepared use of real pain – such as suspensions, where the celebrant is literally suspended in the air by hooks inserted through their skin – it requires honesty, trust, and good communication among the ritualists.

Erotic play can be entirely pleasant, or involve a small component of pain, or more frequently, frustration. Straight erotic stimulation is effective, but the addition of an element of tease raises the power of the response exponentially, as the pleasure is enhanced through anticipation, making the ultimate release more potent.

There is an oracular working that is used by some groups, that could be considered to be the ultimate expression of this. It involves two or more participants, one of whom is to be the oracle. In sacred space, the naked oracle lies down on a raised platform – a massage table is excellent for this – and the other participants begin gently stroking his or her body, starting at the extremities and moving towards the core. The aim is to invoke a deeply sensual state of mind through the stroking, to bring the oracle as close to the point of release as possible without taking them over the edge. Naturally, direct contact with the genitals, nipples, anus, etc. is to be avoided, but in all other respects the stroking is extremely sexual, slow and languorous. Ideally, the oracle is brought to the point where they are straining for release – sometimes it is necessary to restrain them briefly until they cool down – again and again. Suitable music is played throughout, and in most groups there are chants and incantations appropriate to the Mysteries practiced by the group. This combination finally culminates in a transcendent metamorphosis, where the oracle becomes suddenly totally calm and begins to speak with oracular prophecies. In this state, they can bear messages from the Gods and ancestors, or respond to questions asked by one of the other participants. When the oracular session is complete, the others then resume stroking the oracle, this time allowing the process to continue to an orgasmic release.

While a very potent technique, it is important to realize that it is very taxing for all the participants, and very difficult to maintain focus on, as all of the participants are likely to become extremely sexually aroused and will struggle to maintain their self-control. This is why some practitioners prefer the related technique of eroto-comatose lucidity, which achieves the same end through repeated orgasms to the point of physical exhaustion via oral or manual stimulation.

All of these practices invoke a powerful visceral full-body response from the recipient or recipients, and it is this powerful emotion, be it ecstasy, pain, joy or sorrow, or even anger, that turns the cauldron.

The Great Rite

While the potency of erotic touching is not to be ignored, as evidenced above, the potential of sex as a visceral trigger is quite unique, because in many ways the simulation of actual sex in a way that provokes a visceral response can almost be more powerful than actual sex itself.

Many Pagans use a libation as the final act of a ritual before closing the sacred space, consecrating or otherwise empowering a sacrament of wine and cake (or equivalent) to share among the participants. In Wicca and some other forms of Witchcraft this is often done in the form of the symbolic Great Rite, where the tools – a chalice and either a blade or a wand – represent the sexual organs of the Lord and Lady, brought together in union.

As I mentioned in the section on using sex as a trigger, it has been my experience for many years, that when done with passion and in a visceral manner by the celebrants, the "symbolic" rite ceases to be symbolic, not only for them, but for all present. Over the years in my coven workings, and more recently when demonstrating this as part of the Visceral Magick workshops I have taught, it has been quite obvious that not only do the celebrants achieve a state of union that is as complete an overpowering as if they were physically engaging in coitus, but that every person present is not merely witnessing the act, but actively participating in it, in every sense but the physical. This understandably results in a powerful, emotional and visceral response in everyone present, and as the final act in a ritual designed to manifest something in our world, it is unparalleled.

Vision Quests

Vision quests, also known as pathworkings or guided meditations, are generally seen as a useful but fairly passive technique, mainly used to introduce students to the deities the group works with, or the realms they will encounter in the rites. One of the really cool things about vision quests is that, no matter how weakly you can interact with them, they will affect you on some level or another.

Even if you are unable to engage with the vision quest at all, and can just listen to the words spoken by the facilitator, this level of interaction can affect you at a subconscious level. But if you are able to go into any level of trance state and visualize what is being described, the effect is much more profound. Finally, a deep trance and visceral connection will enable you to interact fully at every level, at which point the experience is as real and effective as any physical experience, sometimes more so.

Techniques to Trigger Visceral Experiences

*I*nstant triggers are great to kick-start the process, and to enable people of varying ability to work together. But the real work of personal spiritual evolution is done by the experiences that result from more long-term triggers that help to develop the mental and spiritual "muscles" to really make the most of visceral magick.

These are the forms in which visceral magick comes to us from our ancestors, and while some are technique-oriented, most are lore and story based. All use technique to some extent, but that technique is mostly to do with the way we receive the lore and internalize it, so that we can let it build up inside us to create and facilitate the amazing visceral experiences that are literally life-changing.

Eating The Gods

Many cultures have religious practices that are referred to by anthropologists as Theophagy – literally "eating the Gods". Ranging from actual acts of cannibalism, where respected enemies slain in battle or recently departed relatives are consumed in ritual meals, to more symbolic acts such as the Catholic mass, these rites take the "you are what you eat" approach that is an extension of the hunter eating the heart and liver of the animals they kill to give them the strength and bravery of the creature.

Obviously, in modern western culture these acts are of the symbolic variety, but that does not mean they didn't originate in actual acts of eating the flesh of other humans – after all, our ancestors practiced human sacrifice. But for legal and ethical reasons, the modern practitioner is going to be practicing theophagy in the form of the libation, houzle, or by ingesting the body fluids of a partner.

The libation or houzle has a direct correlation to the Catholic Mass, and it is generally accepted - by Pagans at least – that the mass is a Christianized version of the Pagan libation. In the ceremony of the mass, the wafer and wine are not merely symbolic representations of the body and blood of Christ, as it is in protestant communion rites, but through the magical act of transubstantiation, becomes the actual body and blood of their savior, and it is through the ingesting of this god-flesh that they achieve salvation. It is a literal interpretation of "taking Christ into their body and heart".

Modern neo-Pagans, especially Wiccans, use a fairly ceremonial interpretation of the libation, where the energy of the ritual and the invocations that has not been used up in the working itself, is "poured" into the cake and ale (or whatever is being used for the libation) and shared among the participants. In fact, in Gardnerian and Alexandrian Wicca, this act of libation actually signals the end of the interaction of the Lord and Lady, as the remnants of the essence that has been invoked into the circle is placed in the chalice for all to share.

Libation among traditional crafters – sometimes called the Houzle after Cornish practice – could be considered to fall somewhere between the symbolic practice of protestant Christians and neo-Pagans and the transubstantiation of Catholics, because it really works both angles of the technique. The drink and food that is shared represents the blood and bone of the ancestors in a way that is more than symbolic, as it reaffirms the tangible link of the crafter with their ancestors, including the Gods, who are often seen as the most ancient ancestors. The drink is, for crafters, always an alcoholic beverage, frequently dark ale or mead, though red wine is also acceptable. Occasionally an appropriate spirit is used, such as whisky (or whiskey) for those following a Celtic path. Even Gardner, in his Book of Shadows, refers to the libation being wine, spirit, or something that "has life in it". The reason for this is partly the value of the drink as an intoxicant, promoting an altered state of consciousness, but also because the "life" of an alcoholic drink is better able to absorb and carry the magical energy or life force of the Gods, in much the same way that a universal accumulator such as gold chloride or chamomile tea stores the life-force or magical energy of the practitioner.

A toast is usually offered up to the Horned Lord, and to the ancestors, but the old-school way of doing this is to dip the bread into the brew, symbolizing the bone immersed in the blood. This calls upon the symbolism of the "bone ladder", or the body of practices that crafters use, being empowered or "enfleshed" by the River of Blood, which represents the lore and wisdom of the ancestors that is carried in the stories, philosophy, and the actual blood/DNA of the current practitioners, that has been passed down to them by those who came before. At this point, the symbolic libation, linking as it does to all of this imagery that is central to the transmission of the Tradition itself, becomes something more, as it triggers a visceral response in the crafter that stirs the ancestral memories and promotes a "remembering" of the lore and the connection to the ancestors, enflaming the blood in a very real, if spiritually oriented way.

Raising the Forge Flame and Summoning the Ancestors

This is a deceptively simple pair of techniques. The first part involves raising the Forge Flame from the center of the earth into our bodies, and the second part involves calling in the Ancestors.

As with most of the techniques that are designed to trigger visceral experiences, this technique relies on a deep understanding of the associated lore, another reason why it is important for the crafter to immerse themselves in the stories, myths and philosophy of their path, and not just focus on the raw techniques. The techniques by themselves will bring results, but it is the wisdom and understanding from experiencing the lore directly and viscerally that lends power to the techniques, augmenting their potency and effect in a way that furthers the visceral response, itself amplifying the results. In this way the combination of lore and praxis become a sort of "particle accelerator" for magick, as the lore augments the praxis, which amplifies the visceral response, which brings the lore to life, which enhances the praxis, and so on.

The lore associated with this practice is the lore of the Interior Sun. In Welsh Celtic myths, while Bel or Belli was the Sun in the Sky, there was a counterpart known as Celli, who was the Black Sun at the heart of planet earth. The concept of a hollow earth is fairly common in ancient cultures, and often associated with the stories about Faeries, but some of the oldest stories from the British Isles refer to the hollow enclosure containing a black sun that was the source of all magick. For my Welsh Celtic ancestors, this Black Sun, Celli, was the consort of the goddess Ced, who was the enclosure itself, and could be considered the Underworld counterpart of Cerridwen, according to various practitioners.

In the lore as it applies to magical practice, this Black Sun is often seen as the Forge, and so the technique that is most strongly associated with it is the technique of raising the Forge Fire. This is a practice that is both useful as a way of raising energy for spell-crafting and charging of tools and talismans, but is also especially valuable for its powerful visceral effect on the practitioner, both by triggering many of the visceral experiences, but through its direct effect on the Cauldrons and upon the crafter's capacity to respond viscerally to the various triggers and practices. In fact, I would go so far as to say that this is the one indispensable technique that all practitioners who wish to explore visceral magick must work with.

The technique itself is very simple, and is perfected in two parts. First the practitioner develops skill in raising the Forge Fire, and then adds the act of summoning the Ancestors to complete the technique.

To raise the Forge Fire, stand in the center of your workspace, with all your normal wards and guardians in place (to create your normal sacred space), and turn your attention to your heart. Feel the flickering flame of life force, and start to fan this flame by using the technique that is often referred to as "bellows breathing". This involves imagining that the space you are in is a giant bellows, and instead of inhaling and exhaling, when you breathe it is the bellows pushing air into your body, and then sucking the air out again. In this way you stoke the flame in your heart into a bright fire, which you then begin to send down through your body and into the earth. With each exhalation, you send your heart (or hearth) fire deeper and deeper, until it encounters the great Forge Fire that is the Interior Sun.

At this point, you begin to draw the fire back up towards yourself with every inhaled breath, bringing with it the forge fire from the Black

Sun. Draw this fire up into your heart, where it spreads out throughout your body, causing your blood to boil.

Practice this technique regularly, until you have mastered it, and then it is time to summon the Ancestors. For this you make a few extra preparations. First, place your stang, staff, or other representation of the World Tree or Bilé Tree in the center of your working space, with your hearthstone and Ancestral Skull at its base, facing west. Take water, and drizzling it from the eastern edge of your space, draw a ley-line to the western edge, crossing the base of the Tree, and flick water out to the west, beyond the edge of your space, into infinity. Standing in front of your Tree facing west, raise the Forge Fire as described. When you get to the point where your blood is boiling with the energy of the Forge Fire, call down the cold pale blue fire from the stars above and mix it with the red Forge Fire, turning the whole a deep blue, and extending your arms on either side (forming a cross with the ley-line you created, and also on the vertical plane with the Tree), extend the energy out in all directions as you call out mentally, emotionally and physically to the ancestors, asking them to come and claim you as their own.

My experience with this technique, both in my own practice and working with the members of my coven, has been quite profound. The response of the ancestors, when the practitioner is ready, is swift and powerful, and in the coven situation, I have witnessed the ancestors marking the coven hearthstone with a symbol, stamped in gold, for each covener that was claimed. Naturally, we keep a record of the symbols, and use them to empower our spell-crafting. This is a technique that can be repeated until success is achieved, and then repeated whenever the need is felt, to reaffirm the connection with the ancestors.

Road To Elfame

There are many folk tales – and folk songs – about journeys to the Land of the Faeries, all replete with warnings about eating Faerie-fare and the way time passes very quickly. From the tale of Thomas The Rhymer to the Preiddeu Annwn, stories tell of the fascination that fairies and mortals have for each other, and the mischief that is wrought in the pursuit of that fascination. Shakespeare wrote about it in A Midsummer Night's Dream, making good use of the myth of Puck, or Robin Goodfellow, and this storytelling tradition has continued with the fantasy novels of Julian May (The Many-Colored Land) and Jim Butcher (The Dresden Files).

The machinations of modern fiction aside, most of the old tales tell of unusual circumstances that enable a traveler to "part the veil" and both see and interact with the Faerie realm. Some are simple, such as being dragged backwards through a hawthorn hedge, and some involve being at a particular location on a particular date and time, such as Alderney Edge or Wayland's Smithy, and some involve a ritual. But the common denominator is that either by accident or design, the traveler is properly prepared and in the right state of mind to make the transition.

Traditional Crafters frequently have ways of entering sacred space that mimic these classic modes of entry, whether it is the besom bridge that echoes the knife's edge or glass bridge of Germanic myth that joins the mortal realm to the realm of the Gods, or the leftward spin some crafters employ on entering the space that mimics the climbing over the stile that is used in rural areas to cross a hedgerow into a field.

All of these techniques, when performed in a visceral way, create a very real change in the practitioner and the space, literally placing them in an altered state of consciousness and taking them between the worlds. This is often recognized by the apparent "thickening" of the atmosphere in the place, accompanied by a sense of "now-ness", where past, present and future co-exist in a timeless "now". It is an experience that, once achieved, is never forgotten.

By itself, the "all space is here, all time is now" transformation is profound enough, and for traditional crafters is an essential part of the preparation for ritual and magick. But when you add specific journeying techniques, such as backing into the spindle or Bilé Tree, it can become transcendental. This place between the worlds, or "over the hedge" is also the perfect environment for calling upon and interacting with Gods and other entities, including the ancestors.

As if that weren't enough, determined crafters can take advantage of the myths associated with specific locations, and use their skill in the above techniques, along with the descriptions of how it should be approached for the site, to slip between the worlds at points where our ancestors were wont to do so, which is a great way of encountering the Spirit of Place of a sacred site, or interacting with the place's associated Mystery.

Plant Allies

The use of psychoactive plants in shamanic practice is common worldwide. We hear a lot these days about the South American

Ayahuasca vine, as well as Peyote and San Pedro. These are the "flavors of the moment", but it should be remembered that the indigenous magical practices of Europe have their plant allies too.

Many books have been written about the legendary properties of the lethal Amanita Muscaria, or Fly Agaric. This classic red-with-white-spots mushroom features in myths, fairy tales and even video games, and it is often seen as the original magick mushroom. But there is a tradition of using many other plants too, from Mother Redcap's safer cousin, Psilocybe or Liberty Cap, through various herbs like skullcap and wormwood, to the notorious flying ointment described in the Witch Trials. It cannot be denied that these plants, when used carefully and responsibly, can promote and enhance visceral experiences in conjunction with the other rites and techniques. Indeed, perhaps the most famous visceral experience attributed to classical witchcraft, the Witches' Flight to the Sacred Mountain, is usually depicted as being the result of either flying ointment, Mother Redcap, or the ergot fungus that is the precursor of LSD.

The key here, of course, is that these allies are used responsibly, as enhancers, not indiscriminately as a short-cut or replacement for hard study and practice. Most of these substances have been at least tried by various counter-cultures for recreational purposes, and while many of them are safe, there is still the issue of legality.

Luckily, the plants that are most useful for the student of visceral magick are still (for now, at least) legal, and fairly safe. Salvia Divinorum, or Diviner's Sage, is as safe as any plant can be, though it has been tried and rejected by many revelers as not being useful as a party drug. It has a reputation of being hallucinogenic in stronger doses, but about half of recreational users either get no response or are disappointed that the experience is "not fun." Basically, for the crafter, the key is that this is a plant that enhances the trance experience – in other words, you need to be competent at using some technique for entering a trance state before the salvia makes a difference. When used properly, it will enhance any trance technique, so it can be of great value to divination (hence the name) as well as journey work and exploring the Mysteries.

Wormwood is the classic dreamer's herb, used in dream pillows and divination incense even in New Age stores in modern times. However, it is underrated, despite being the legendary ingredient that creates the "green fairy" effect in that most Bohemian of beverages, absinthe.

Of course, in real absinthe, the secret is in the combination of herbs, not just the wormwood, but Artemesia Absinthum does have a well-deserved reputation for provoking prophetic and magical dreams, and used in conjunction with other magical techniques can help the student achieve a visceral experience that they were perhaps just falling short of without the wormwood.

When it comes to the more famous magical herbs, we have to bear in mind that their usefulness is offset by their illegal status and their toxicity. Fly Agaric was the cause of death for Robert Cochrane (author of what came to be known as the 1734 letters), after he overdosed on them in a ritual – the jury is out as to whether this was accidental or deliberate. Flying ointment is also a dangerous substance, though effective, including some fairly toxic plants such as henbane, deadly nightshade and aconite in its recipe. Properly blended in the right proportions, the recipe's toxic components cancel each other out to some extent, but it is still a risky tool to use, and not recommended without proper supervision from an experienced practitioner, and an accurate recipe (as far as I know, none of the published versions give the correct specifics of what and how much to use).

Visceral Experiences

Nightmares of Lilith

Despite the name, this actually has very little to do with Lilith, other than the fact that she is the "Bringer of Nightmares". It is also a visceral experience that cannot be consciously triggered, but instead seems to be a spontaneous part of the opening up of the visceral intelligence. You can't plan for it, but there is a good chance that you will experience it at some point in your spiritual journey.

Most people are caught unawares by this experience. Even those who have heard of it and know details about it tend to find its appearance to be a complete surprise. The Nightmares tend to take the form of bloody nightmares that frequently involve either more gore than you could usually handle, or distressing events that have the same overall effect. My own experience, for example, involved a lot of blood and internal organs, but I have heard of other accounts where the dreamer spent several nights killing kittens in various ways – she was a cat lover, so this was as distressing to her as my own organ-spewing dreams.

These dreams tend to continue over a course of about a week, ending only when the dreamer either surrenders to the experience or rejects it completely. They tend to have little or no clues to their esoteric nature, until you reach the end of the series, when they invariably end with a profound encounter with the Black Goddess, or a cultural equivalent.

In my case, the dreams began with a fairly standard – for me – nightmare. I should point out that I am a little strange (in case you hadn't already guessed), and I actually enjoy nightmares because I see them as my own personal horror movies. This one was a little different, though, because my nightmares are not normally gory, and it became more and more bloody as the dream progressed. It took place in a railway yard... lots of tracks, engines, rolling stock – mostly freight containers, though there were some passenger carriages. I was with someone I didn't recognize, who was being pursued, and for most of the dream we never saw the pursuers, but went from near-escape to near-escape in classic horror-movie style, seeing a shadow or feeling/hearing a presence without actually seeing directly what was after us.

Of course, the time came when the pursuers – zombies – broke through and ripped my anonymous companion to shreds, and then the dream became more frantic. In the end I was cornered, but I literally tore two of the zombies apart with my hands to make my escape, and the dream ended.

The next night involved a road-trip of some sort, with my fellow coveners on board. We were going from town to town searching for something, and one by one the others on the bus were taken out, until there were only myself and one other left. At this point we found the entrance to a cave system, and on entering the caves, we found an ancient temple at the far side of a labyrinth, where some of our missing companions were trying to reconstruct the ancient ritual that used to be performed there. They had robes and regalia that were apparently copies of the originals, but were having little success. This resulted in large bat-like creatures carrying them off, one by one, until only the Mistress of the coven was left. By this time, I had found a side cave, where the original robes and regalia were hidden, and the three of us were able to complete the ritual and banish the bat-like creatures, though not without the unnamed companion being torn to shreds by the creatures.

The next few nights involved me travelling from place to place in a car, on foot, and finally on a motorbike. The towns I encountered were practically uninhabited, post-apocalyptic, but each night there were a handful of people, often being hunted by a psychopath or creature of some sort.

The final night was different, though. I was riding my motorbike in torrential rain, and arrived in the center of a one-horse town that appeared deserted. Standing before a billboard that I could not read in an abandoned bus station, I suddenly realized where I needed to be (without consciously knowing where that was). I mounted the bike, turned around and headed out of town through the rain. It was late, around midnight.

After battling the bike through the wet weather for what seemed like an eternity, I found myself outside a run-down house filled with bikers partying. I went inside, to find that as I entered the room it went silent – not in the "stranger enters the bar" way, but a respectful silence as everyone acknowledged me. As I went through to the next room, the people there fell into the same respectful silence, while the room I left erupted into the life and noise of the party once again. Room after room I encountered the same, until I finally came upon a room that was empty except for what appeared to be a huge, oversized motorbike. The door behind me closed, and I realized that there was somebody reclining on the bike, a huge "Venus of Willendorf" proportioned female whose age I could not discern. She was naked, covered in deep black tribal tattoos, though her skin was white, and the tattoos were moving. She was, of course, the Black Mother, and I climbed up onto the motorbike and was embraced by her – this was at once a sexual and non-sexual encounter, resulting in the tattoos that covered her also covering me.

The key to all of this was that each nightmare came to a satisfactory conclusion once I surrendered to it. When I overcame my revulsion and did what was necessary, I was able to move forward. Finally, I met the Black Goddess, and knowing I was going to my doom, I embraced her and everything she represents.

Since that final night, I have encountered Her in my dreams, but She does not waste Her time with the gore any more. Instead she gives me dreams that inspire my waking rituals, and my writing. Although the Nightmares of Lilith are a powerful visceral tool for developing your abilities, they are above all a sign that you are on the right track. On the flip-side, they are a challenge that tests your ability to surrender to the bloody events you encounter, to do what is necessary. I believe there are parallels with eastern exercises, such as the Buddhist "contemplating the self as a rotting corpse".

One important thing to note is that the Nightmares of Lilith are not pleasant – they deliberately target your boundaries by making use of imagery and actions that repulse you personally. For this reason most people reject them when they occur, and they go away. I do not know for sure if, once rejected, they will ever return, but I believe that they will cycle around again after a time, when your other efforts at spiritual evolution bring you to another place that is conducive to invoking them.

The key to completing this experience is truly to surrender yourself to it. This is not only traumatic at the time, but it will have knock-on effects. Some of these are going to be the mental and spiritual aspects of coping with the experience, but the plus side is that there are few experiences that will bring your visceral magick into manifestation better than the Nightmares. Once they have been experienced, it is as if the connection between the "rational" mind and the visceral intellect are hard-wired, allowing a huge leap in ability to be made. This increase in ability can be made without the Nightmares, but they really do act as a kind of short-cut.

Merlin's Madness

One of the – to me at least – most fascinating pieces of the Arthurian legend, is the tale of the Madness of Merlin. The Vita Merlini, written in Latin around 1150 AD by Geoffrey of Monmouth, is an account of Merlin going completely loopy and running off into the forest to live with the beasts after the death of Arthur. It describes Merlin in terms that are very reminiscent of the Wild Man of the Forest, and it is this madness that brings about Merlin's greatest powers of prophecy.

As a technique for evoking visceral experiences, Merlin's Madness leaves a lot to be desired. It is certainly an effective path, but one that is fraught with problems. The main problem is that the term "madness" is not given lightly to this technique – the student who follows this path in modern times is likely to be diagnosed as insane, and to be locked up in a psychiatric ward, as the key to the technique is to completely separate yourself from reality. It is a simple technique, but the effects are likely to last for three to six months, and without experienced caregivers who know what is going on, that is too long to avoid some good Samaritan calling for psychiatric intervention.

Although I don't recommend using it, I will describe the basics. Essentially the crafter divorces themself from reality by starting to question everything. You literally question whether what you see before you is really there, including your own image when you look in a mirror. At first this involves just asking the question, but if you do it thoroughly enough for long enough, the questions take hold of you, and bit by bit your grasp on reality is loosened, until you enter a state of total dissociation with the mundane world. Of course, as a magical practitioner, the concept of blind in this world means sighted in the other, and so your barriers to perceiving the non-physical planes are removed, and your perception of what is real is not only open to question, but many of the things you perceive are not there as far as anyone else is concerned. I cannot stress how invigorating this is from a magical perspective, which is why it was a respected technique for shamans for so many millennia, but it does not work with a job, a normal family life, or any interaction with modern society. Even in medieval times, practitioners would take themselves off into the wilderness or to a hermitage or monastery, where their behavior was not witnessed by others, or where it was considered to be an appropriate part of their spiritual path. It is next to impossible to achieve this safely in the 21st century.

Encountering Dark Visions (Hanging on the Tree)

The first time I experienced hanging on the tree was the year I spent as Sacred King for the coven I trained with. At Lammas, the initiates used their cords as cable-tows, placing a noose at one end around their neck and tying the other end to the forks of the stang, sitting at the foot of the stang/tree as the dedicants and guests trod the mill around them, and the Mill Wife dropped flour mixed with crushed eggshell (aka graveyard dust) on their heads. During the Mill, we descended into the Underworld for chthonic experiences until the mill was reversed and we were all brought back up again. As Sacred King, I had a loaf of bread on my lap (the "scapegoat"), the idea being that the gods would either take my life in sacrifice, or accept the bread as a suitable substitute.

I found the experience very profound. I walked through an underground tunnel, accompanied by a non-human entity, until I arrived at a great bronze gate. I don't remember exactly how I got through the gate, but on the other side the tunnel was partially flooded, and I had to swim until we arrived at a silver gate. This gate slid up and down, and I had to dive down under the water to get through, but on the other side I continued my journey along a narrow path that skirted the crater of an underground volcano – fire, fumes and smoke everywhere, all lit up by red flame and glowing magma.

Finally I reached a golden trapdoor, set in the ground, and it opened to reveal loam, loose dirt. I had to dive into it and literally claw my way down ever deeper through the dark earth, until I came out into a great cavern, literally a huge space at the center of the earth, with about a ten-foot gap between where I clung to a rocky outcrop and the surface of the black interior sun that occupied the center. A vaguely feminine form appeared to be swimming in the surface of this black sun, and she beckoned me to join her. I realized that the only way I could do so was to make the "salmon-leap" of faith, and summoning my courage, I did so.

I found myself "swimming" in the sun's surface too, though all too aware that the heat was consuming me. At this point I was made aware that the Gods had chosen to accept me as the sacrifice, and that I would not be returning from the journey. Fear, for myself and my family gripped me, but as I floated in the embrace of the Dark Lady who held me, I found a calmness descended over me, and I surrendered to my fate. At that exact moment, She told me that because I had accepted my demise, I was free to return, and I found myself floating directly up and out, until I became aware of myself lying under the stang, in the arms of the Coven Mistress... apparently I had not been breathing for some time. Ever since – and this happened several years ago – I have been very aware that, while I returned whole and complete, there is still, somehow, a part of me floating on the surface of that interior sun, and I can very quickly return there whenever I desire. That night was the start of my experiencing magical energy in a very physical way, when my magical and mundane lives ceased to be separate.

Part Four

The Cauldron of Wisdom

Formal Training and Divine Intercession

*I*t is said that the Cauldron of Wisdom can only be tipped by formal training and the Will of the Gods. Ultimately this is saying that the final stage of the visceral process requires an act of surrender, to open yourself up to the Gods and Ancestors, and let them in. Where the formal training comes in is the role of the teacher as facilitator.

Some subjects can be taught by rote. Language is often taught this way, both vocabulary and grammar, and I certainly suffered through history lessons where we learnt lists of facts by rote. But the Mysteries, especially where visceral magick is concerned, are experiential. It isn't enough to know the stories, to recognize the traits and descriptions of the Gods, to have memorized rituals and incantations. The lore must become a living, breathing thing within your heart, and that requires you to experience the stories, encounter the gods, and become part of the lore itself. A good teacher provides opportunities to have these experiences, priming us with just enough fact and philosophy to enable us to grasp it fully, without "spoiling the surprise" or short-circuiting the process.

As one of my mentors once told me, if we are given a bunch of facts, told the theory behind the techniques, and taught by rote, we do not own the knowledge, and it has no chance of developing into wisdom. But if we experience the lore for ourselves, discover the mechanism of the techniques and explore the philosophy behind them, we take ownership of the knowledge, and don't have to take it as read on someone else's say so. That is the reason behind vows of secrecy and silence - to avoid short-circuiting the student's progress by giving them too much information before they have the relevant experience – and why nobody can claim copyright or overall ownership of a tradition, or that they have "given" it to someone else. We all discover every piece for ourselves, though others may guide and facilitate our learning process. So we each own our Mystery, and it cannot be taken away from us.

The traditional way that divine intervention is expressed, especially in the context of the three cauldrons, is Imbas, or the "Divine Frenzy". This is where the bard speaks in the poetic language of the Gods, divinely inspired. In ancient days this would be translated by experienced priests/druids, or it would be intelligible but couched in riddles. Ultimately, it is the ability to allow the gods to speak and act directly through us, to become "as one with the Gods". Note that this is not a permanent or long-term state of being, but something that exists under special circumstances for a brief span of time. I am certain that it can last longer, but I am equally certain that it does not need to – that brief spark of the divine in our words, our eyes and our power is enough.

Instant Visceral Triggers

Invocation and the Ancient Art of Ritual Possession

*T*he information contained here comes from many sources. Practically every teacher I have studied with has contributed in some way to what I am sharing, plus there is a lot of stuff that is the result of my own exploration and experimentation. I hope you find it useful.

What is Invocation

The Pagan community has some interesting interpretations of the word "invoke". A lot of that is due to the word being intrinsically linked to the concept of deity, and that word means different things to different people. The word "invoke" literally means "to call in ("invoce", Latin), and is paired in most magical traditions with "evoke", which literally means "to call out", but is usually taken as meaning "to call forth". Many Pagans use the terms interchangeably, but there is a significant difference to the serious practitioner.

When we invoke, we call the deity into ourselves or another

practitioner, while evocation usually involves calling the deity into a prepared space or object rather than a person. This can also be performed with other entitles, such as angelic or demonic beings, and in ceremonial magick it is the entities who are not necessarily friendly that are summoned by the act of evocation.

For the modern crafter, evocation is most often used when the presence or energy of the deity is required, but not direct interaction from them. This is the preferred practice of those who perform rites for the community, as it is gentler, easier, and less likely to freak anyone out. The big question, of course, is why we call on the deities in the first place.

Some traditions work primarily with the gods of their culture. Wicca, for example, works almost exclusively with the Goddess ("the Lady") and Her Consort, the Horned Lord. She is called on using the technique of "Drawing Down the Moon" pretty much in every rite, while the Horned Lord is called, via "Drawing Down the Sun", at appropriate times.

Those of us who work outside of Wicca often do things a little differently. If you believe, as I do, that Witchcraft is a practice rather than a religion, then you are likely to work within the religious constructs of your culture. So Italian Witches, the Stregha, work with the saints of Catholic Christianity, as do many other regional forms of witchcraft or shamanism. Wicca is a religion that openly accepts the practice of witchcraft within it, but most other religions see witchcraft as at least heretical. As a person who practices Witchcraft within a Welsh Celtic Pagan spirituality that is based on and connected to the spirituality of my ancestors, I usually call on those ancestors for "everyday" things, saving the Gods for special occasions and "the big stuff". For me, that usually means that I call on the Gods and Goddesses at the major festivals - we work the Mysteries rather than celebrate the seasons at our festivals - but rarely for spell-crafting or healing work.

Of course, the most interesting part of this for others is the techniques themselves, how we invoke our Gods. I've heard many people in the Pagan community describe magick, and spells in particular, as "prayer with props", and I have to say that I heartily disagree with this statement. A prayer is a supplication, a cry for help, or an offering, a way of saying thank you. Spell-crafting and magick in general may make use of these as components, but they are a very different creature indeed.

When you pray to a god, you are sending them a message. But when you invoke, you are calling them to come and interact, and this is a very important difference. Prayer is the tool of the worshipper, who offers up their devotion in return for the favor of their deity. Crafters don't worship their gods, so prayer becomes somewhat superfluous. What we offer our gods is respect and service. We barter with them, make deals, and explore their Mysteries and lore in order to evolve, to become more like them. Invocation is a powerful tool in this evolutionary, experiential process, and there are several methods used by different traditions to accomplish this.

Classical Invocation

The term "invocation" is primarily used with regard to the Ceremonial Magician's technique, as more "rustic" traditions have other names for it, such as being "ridden" or "mounted". Possession has come to be associated with demonic possession, courtesy of movies like "The Exorcist", but it is a term commonly used among ethnic practitioners.

But the classical term comes with a classical technique. I like to call the classical format the three-part invocation - I don't know whether this was ever a formal way of doing it, but looking at the wording of classical "prayers" of invocation has led me to extrapolate a specific way of working based on this three-fold technique. Appropriately, there are three ways of looking at these techniques, and it is best to start with the words used.

If you look at any of the ancient invocations, you will generally see a format that consists of three parts. The words start by calling on the deity, trying to get their attention. The invocation begins by calling on the deity by one or more names, titles or epithets. Here is an example from the Golden Dawn's Invocation of the Bornless One:

> "Thee I invoke, the Bornless one.
> Thee, that didst create the Earth and the Heavens:
> Thee, that didst create the Night and the day.
> Thee, that didst create the darkness and the Light..."

In this case, the titles, etc., are replaced by a list of the deity's achievements. The celebrant then moves to the second phase, where they speak directly to the deity as present before them, often citing their authority for calling on them:

> "I am _____ Thy Prophet, unto Whom Thou didst
> commit Thy Mysteries, the Ceremonies of _____:
> Thou didst produce the moist and the dry, and that which
> nourisheth all created Life.
> Hear Thou Me, for I am the Angel of Apophrasz
> Osorronophris: this is Thy True Name, handed down to the
> Prophets of _____..."

Finally, the celebrant speaks as the deity, signifying that the
invocation is complete and successful:

> "I am He! the Bornless Spirit! having sight in the Feet: Strong,
> and the Immortal Fire!
> I am He! the Truth!
> I am He! Who hate that evil should be wrought in the World!
> I am He, that lightningeth and thundereth.
> I am He, from whom is the Shower of the Life of Earth:
> I am He, whose mouth flameth:
> I am He, the Begetter and Manifester unto the Light:
> I am He, the Grace of the World:
> "The Heart Girt with a Serpent" is My Name!"

In a ritual where the deity is being called to share words of wisdom,
it is common for the last words of the invocation to be the words of
the deity, as the hardest part of the process after opening yourself up is
letting the deity use your mouth. But we'll talk about that later.

The key to all this verbiage is that, besides its sheer commonsense
(get their attention, invite them in, listen to what they say), it allows for
an interplay of energy to take place. Invocations that involve a formal
spoken component are nearly always conducted by a group rather
than a solitary individual. The natural rhythm of the piece allows an
interplay of energy to occur, where the celebrant, standing in the center
or at the focal point of the rite, intones the first part of the invocation,
extending energy towards the participants in order to "light the fire".
The participants then intone the second section, taking the energy
from the celebrant and amplifying it, and then each participant returns
the full amount of the energy to the celebrant. This amplified energy
is then used by the celebrant to raise their vibration to the point where
the deity can step in, by using the visualization described below, or a
variant of it. The final step is when the celebrant, now inhabited by
the deity, speaks the words of the deity and encompasses the other

participants in the energy brought in with the deity, thus raising their energies so that they too can perceive and interact with their God.

The visualization is the key to this type of invocation, and the one I give here is not specific to any particular magical lodge or group, but is rather a generic one I have formulated for teaching purposes.

The celebrant begins by visualizing themself as starting to grow larger as they begin the invocation. With every word, they grow larger and larger, until by the end of the first section, they see themselves as being so large that planet earth is a footstool, on which they are standing. From this expanded vantage point, they look out from the center of a huge circle comprising every deity of their pantheon. As the words of the participants, and their amplified energy, lifts them up, the visualization becomes something more, and the deity they are calling steps towards them, and then takes up a position immediately behind them. The full impact of the amplified energy raises their vibration to a point where the deity is able to step forward into them, inhabiting their body, and the celebrant/deity then visualizes shrinking back down to normal size, the celebrant bringing the deity down into the Temple within themself. The deity then speaks the final words of the invocation, and then begins to converse and interact with the participants in order to achieve the goal of the rite.

This technique can be used by a solitary practitioner, but it is somewhat pointless to do so, as you are effectively inviting the deity into a room to converse, and having nobody there to talk to them once they arrive. However, there are three levels of invocation that don't often get talked about in ceremonial circles, though they are more familiar to the practitioners of shamanic or folk magick traditions. These three levels are usually referred to as aspect, contact and possession.

An aspect of a deity is where you draw the energy or potency of the deity into the ritual space, but not the personality or "presence" of the deity themselves. This is a useful tool for augmenting healing, charging tools, amulets or talismans, or bringing in extra energy for some other purpose. In this case, instead of the deity stepping into the celebrant in the above visualization, they merely connect energetically with the celebrant, who then brings down the power as if they were bringing in an extension cord from another room.

A contact with a deity is often described as being like a phone call from the deity - the celebrant can "hear" them and speak with them, but the other participants cannot, so the celebrant relays messages to and fro. This requires less effort and skill to maintain, so it can be a very viable way to work with a group that is new and not used to working together yet.

A possession by a deity is exactly what it sounds like... the deity temporarily takes full control of the celebrant's body and uses it to interact with the other participants.

Contact and Possession

For witches and other crafters, there is a much simpler way of working with contacts and possessions, one that does not require the formality and verbiage of the ceremonial approach. Crafters tend to work their magick from the opposite direction of ceremonialists. Whereas ceremonial magicians place themselves at the center of the universe and draw everything into themselves, crafters tend to go out "between the worlds", and encounter gods and heroes in their own realms. This is also achieved through visualization, but it is a much more natural and easy set of images. The celebrant simply goes into trance state through any one of countless techniques, visualizing themselves in a location that is significant to the deity. The god or goddess shows up, and the celebrant regulates whether this is a contact or possession by controlling how close they are to the deity in the visualization. The important part of this technique is being able to open the gateway at the base of the skull, the traditional entry point for spirits, gods and ancestors. This place at the base of the brain is the most ancient part of the brain, often referred to as the reptilian brain, and it contains our most ancient and basic instincts, ancestral memories, and our connection to all who went before.

It is a good idea, especially if you are new to this, or if you are calling in a deity you are not truly familiar with, to set guards at the gateway. Traditionally a crafter will set their Matron and Patron as gatekeepers, but if you don't have those, you can call on a spirit guide or ancestor, and their task is to make sure that the only entity or entities, who enter that gateway are the ones who are supposed to be there.

Once the visualization of the location is established, the celebrant calls on the deity - this need only be done internally - and when they respond, you will find that as you move closer, you begin to feel a merging taking place, and you will find a point a few feet from the deity where your sense of self is completely overwhelmed, but when you move back away from them, you feel your sense of individuality return to you.

This moving closer and further away is the mechanism for consciously controlling whether you are contacting or possessing, but you will find that there is a natural ebb and flow of the experience, so you will actually experience a range from strong contact to strong possession during the course of the rite.

Shamanic Possession – Being "Mounted"

Many indigenous shamanic practitioners make use of the technique of being "ridden" or "mounted" by their gods. This is a well-known part of Santeria, Voudoun and Ifa religions. It essentially involves going into trance and using the rhythm of drum and/or chant to draw a spirit, ancestor or deity into the celebrant. Many of the tribal cultures allow for this to happen spontaneously in the "congregation", and it is how they pick the ones with aptitude to train further in their Mysteries. Interestingly, the same process can be seen in some of the charismatic denominations of Christianity, such as the ones who speak in tongues, the shakers and snake-handlers.

For the modern western practitioner of Old Craft ways, this can be an effective technique for those already fairly experienced in the other methods. I like to call it the "quickening", after the events in the movie "Highlander", because I found that the scene where McLeod runs on the beach with the stag was a major inspiration for me in developing my own version of this way of interacting with the gods.

Getting into a trance state can be done effectively using a number of techniques, the easiest being the use of drums, dance and chant, but once the celebrant is in a trance, it can be quickly deepened and transformed into a mounting by using this simple technique. Two other participants take up a position close to the celebrant, one right behind each shoulder. Alternating from one side to the other, and using a regular heart-beat rhythm to start with, they begin to alternately whisper the name of the deity. Gradually, they increase the speed and intensity of the whisper, until it becomes obvious that the celebrant has become possessed by that deity.

It is important to bear in mind the nature of the visualization that the celebrant uses during this - they should be visualizing the deity in an appropriate setting, coming ever closer until the possession occurs. However, the nature of the image used will define the nature of the possession. A prime example of this was the first time my coven, Briar Rose, tried this technique. We had chosen to call on Herne, and the celebrant for this occasion visualized Herne as a majestic stag on the moor. You can imagine our reaction when the possession took hold - and it really does "take" very suddenly with this technique - and we found ourselves in the powerful presence of what felt like a fully grown stag in his prime, ready to fight, rut or run. We could even smell his musk, and the presence was very physical, very "weighted". Of course, Herne in this form was not interested in conversing, so we released him and brought the celebrant out of his trance state.

A while later, we tried again, but we were careful to make sure that the celebrant visualized Herne as the Hunter...

Conclusion

So what are the hallmarks of a successful invocation? Well, that depends on what you are aiming for. Participants should be aware of a certain energy about the celebrant while the deity is present - obviously this will vary depending upon the ability of the participant, but they should at least notice there is something different. If the deity is present and interacting, it will show in the eyes, a sort of intensity and otherworldliness that is hard to fake. There are also likely to be subtle differences in mannerisms and posture.

The more shamanic, visceral forms of possession, however, tend to be a lot more obvious. The eyes are much stronger in their intensity than the celebrant's usual gaze, and there is often a curious fluidity to the movements of the body that is hard to describe, but impossible to miss once experienced. The energy and intensity with possessions is much less subtle than with invocations.

Unfortunately, there are some who will fake a possession in order to pursue an agenda or to attract attention to themselves, but with a little experience, they are easy to spot. Primarily, the absence of the energy and intensity are a big giveaway, but even a complete novice can watch out for certain signs. To start with, many who fake a possession do so in order to castigate or demean another participant. I can't say this for certain for all cultures, but certainly with the western pantheons I have never observed a deity putting down someone in public, during a group ritual. The gods always seem to manage to do that in private. Also, deities seem to be very aware of peoples' personal space - I have never seen a deity grope a participant unless there is already an established relationship with them that involves intimacy as a spiritual or magical process, so if the celebrant is touching people inappropriately it is highly likely to be a fake possession. But once you have developed enough ability to sense energy, you will never mistake a fake possession for the real thing.

Incidentally, there is one interesting thing about possessions I have noticed, that appears to have no rhyme or reason, but seems to be fairly universal... if the possession is done standing, the deity will have free rein to move about the sacred space, interacting physically with the participants. But if the celebrant is seated for the possession, while the deity might wave their arms and gesticulate, they will remain seated, and interact only verbally with the participants.

The experience for the celebrant is often profound, though it may be initially confusing. Traditionally it is said that the celebrant will remember nothing of a full possession, but because possession occurs with an ebb and flow of intensity, the end result is that the celebrant often remembers things in a one-person-removed way. I've heard people describe it that the words coming from their own mouths sound like the "waa-waa-waa" sound that adults make in the Peanuts cartoons; and others who experience it the way I do, as if the deity and I are over in a corner having our own conversation, and I hear the words spoken to the other participants by the deity (using my physical mouth) as a conversation across the room that I catch snippets of.

The benefits for the celebrant are on several levels. Firstly, as an act of service to the group, it is a powerful way of expressing your commitment to the path, but there is a very real benefit in that possession is a visceral experience, and regular practice of possession facilitates an increase and evolution of the ability to manifest magick in all areas of life, making all magical acts more powerful and profound.

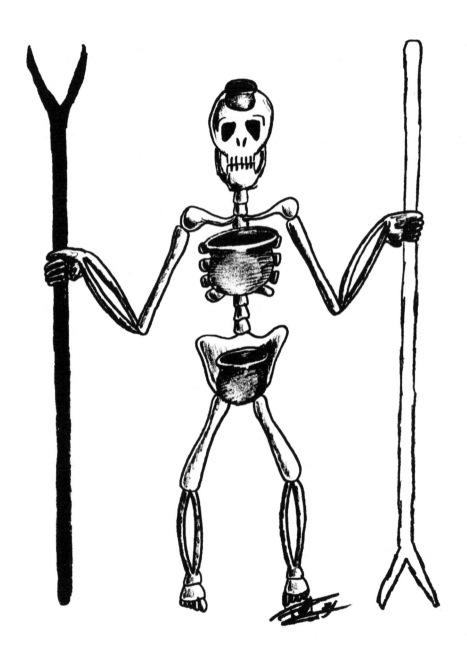

Techniques to Trigger Visceral Experiences

The Sacred King Cycle

For me personally, the Sacred King Cycle was the most important part of my initiatory journey, because it was this that cemented the visceral experience for me, by making me so aware of the process that I couldn't help but figure out what was going on, despite my ignorance of even the existence of the visceral process. All that went before was only clear to me in hindsight after my year as Sacred King brought everything into sharp relief. In other words, if it were not for the Sacred King cycle, this book would not exist.

Many cultures have a Sacred King cycle, or something similar. In Celtic mythology it is at its clearest, and in the Welsh Celtic Mysteries we find what I consider to be its purest expression, though I might just be a little biased on that one. The tales of the Mabinogion include two stories in particular that are central to the Sacred King theme, and all of the stories touch on it in some way. The story of Llew Llaw Gyffes is very important to me, as my path uses it for a large part of our sacred

King cycle as it is applied to our Wheel of the Year, but the story of Mabon, Son of Modron (literally, "Son, son of the Mother"), is the perfect template for the cycle.

Like many versions of this cycle, Mabon is born with nobody knowing who his father is, a child of unknown parentage. At the tender age of three days, he was stolen from his mother. Imprisoned for many years, he was rescued by Arthur's knights, and becoming a knight himself, he slew the great Boar, Tyrch Trwth, and assisted Culhwch in winning his bride, Olwen. After his enforced exile, his rescue and return, and proving himself in the Quest, Mabon eventually becomes a King himself, but not before unknowingly impregnating a young maiden along the way. This theme is fully or partially repeated in the lives of various heroes of Wales, and is echoed in the later romanticized stories of Arthur.

So the key points of the Sacred King's story are that he is born of uncertain parentage, and is either abducted or in some way taken from his mother. The child receives a name under significant circumstances, and after the exile is ended proves himself in some significant way before engendering the hero who will complete the next cycle. Finally, he assumes the role of King, putting away the adventures of his youth to rule his people wisely until he dies.

The cycle can be worked in many ways. My own experience used the story of Llew as a template, and at each of the seasonal rites I explored and experienced various aspects of the cycle. At Imbolc, the birth of Llew was the sub-theme, a counterpoint to the coming of the Child of Promise, the Lord of Light made manifest by the Maid, and at the Spring Equinox I experienced the naming and arming of Llew, important rites of passage for the Celts, conferring the status of manhood. Beltaine was when I experienced the Hieros Gamos, the Sacred Marriage, when the King ensures his successor (in the case of Llew, the successor is his murderer, Geronwy, Bloedwedd's lover, as the story also embodies the Lord of Darkness/Lord of Light duality that is best known as the contest between the Oak King and Holly King). At Midsummer, the King takes up his crown, sacrificing his free will to serve his people, and at Lammas I experienced the death of Llew, entering the Underworld through the portal of the World Tree, before returning to his people. At the Autumn Equinox, I experienced the completion of the cycle as Priest/King, followed by the final descent into the mound at Samhain. Each step had a very profound and deep impact on me, and at each stage I found my visceral response to the energies and imagery got stronger and stronger, and it was shortly after hanging on the Tree at Lammas that I had my nightmares of Lilith, and finally encountered the Dark Mother.

Part Five

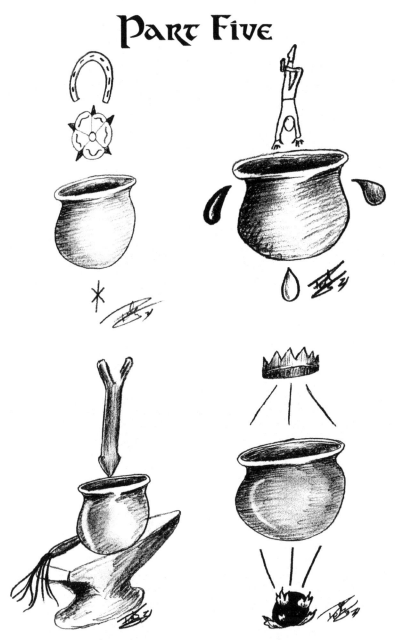

Using Visceral Magick

Spells, Charms and Crafting

One of the most obvious things for me since following the "visceral way" has been the way my spell-crafting has changed. Because my energy-sensing and power raising have become so much more physical, I have found it easier to focus on the physical aspect of each spell – tying knots, casting coins in the well, mixing incenses – and let the energetic part just come naturally. In many ways, I think that any spell-crafting technique will work when done in a visceral manner. I still go through the motions of following the traditional instructions, but I find that the magick part comes naturally and unforced. I've been able to gauge this objectively when teaching workshops on various techniques, because I see the participants responding to the energy in a visceral way as well.

As a result, my crafting has gone back to more traditional methods, such as well working with a handful of silver sixpences, cord magick, and healing by laying on of hands. One of the big problems with traditional spells has been the paucity of instruction – the physical description and words, if any, are provided, but the old grimoires expect the practitioner to have already learnt the energetic and spiritual parts of the spell. For those who are lucky to be in a coven that gives effective training in the "unwritten lore", this is perfectly adequate, but for the solitary practitioner, who may not have access to that kind of training, they are left to "wing it" with what they have gleaned from the superficial coverage most books on the subject provide. It goes without saying that the journey is much easier with a skilled guide to show you the way, but while it is harder to make the journey alone, it is not impossible, and the extra effort is worth it. After all, that is essentially how I have taken this journey, with a combination of insatiable curiosity and good luck. This book will help the solitary practitioner, though it could never replace a teacher who could tailor the approach to the student's specific needs.

You are still going to have to learn the basics of spell-crafting, but once you are experiencing magick viscerally, the energetic and spiritual aspects of the art become second nature, and you can focus your consciousness on the physical part of the spell.

Charging amulets, talismans and charms in general becomes so much easier when you can actually feel the energy that you are using. Selection of appropriate materials or objects is also easier, because the visceral magician can feel the object's resonance with their intent. This means we can do what we are supposed to do as witches or shamen, and let our intuition guide us in selecting the components we need. This also frees us from the restriction of following a table of correspondences, as we can make unconventional choices, confident that our visceral senses are leading us true.

But it is in the greater arena of crafting that visceral magick comes into its own. By being fully and viscerally invested in our magickal experiences, we can move between the worlds and encounter Gods, Ancestors and other spirits much more easily, and interact with the mythic Landscape where our magick is most powerful.

Creating Context
Integrating Visceral Magick with your Tradition

Visceral magick is, I believe, the key that opens the door to the lore and Mysteries of all traditions. Some traditions have kept the techniques and experiences in their training for this, but many have lost them or deliberately dropped them in the name of progress. So how do we go about integrating these practices into the traditions we follow?

First and foremost is the lore. Our Gods and heroes are known to us through the stories our ancestors left for us. Whether we follow a path that is connected to our blood ancestry, or a path that is from a culture other than our own that we feel drawn to, it is the stories that hold the key. So the very first point of integrating visceral magick into any tradition, is to revive the art of storytelling.

Whether you have someone who is skilled at telling stories, or you take turns reading the stories from a good source, it is vital that practitioners get to hear the stories of their Gods and ancestors. Whatever your culture or pantheon, there will be tales of slain and risen gods, sacred kings, journeys to the underworld and initiatory tales. These are the stories that can trigger visceral experiences, inhabit our dreams, and provoke strong emotions that can turn those cauldrons.

Look at the techniques of your tradition. Chances are there are several designed to bring practitioners into a trance state, and they should be used regularly, and in conjunction with the stories, to facilitate the process. Some of the stories may include techniques or actions that are themselves visceral triggers, so where you notice something in a tale that might be one of these, try it out. Work on recreating the actions or techniques in a form that is consistent with your regular practice, and be prepared to spend some time experimenting and tweaking the techniques until you get the desired results.

Look at the history of your tradition, and the culture from which it derives. Are there techniques described that look like they might be visceral or trance techniques that are no longer used? If they are safe, dust them off and try them out. If they are not safe, then either see if you can make them safe, or try them out with observers/catchers who can take care of any issues if they go wrong. I don't advocate doing unsafe things for the hell of it, but if you believe that the results may be worth the risk, that is your call, not mine.

Look to the cosmology of your tradition for clues about visceral experiences and ways of crafting. Frequently a story about a magical event can be turned into an effective crafting – there are literally thousands of examples of this from Ancient Egypt, in the Greek Magical Papyri. Most traditional sex magick rituals stem from the tales of the union of the Gods, and as we have already discussed, sex is a powerful visceral trigger.

Above all, look for the components of your lore, practice and mythology that evoke strong emotional responses, as these are the very things you are looking to make use of.

Facilitating the Experiences in Others

Of course, it is one thing to work through this for yourself. But if you are a coven or group leader, then you need to be able to share the process with others. This is really what is at the core of a traditional crafting path, from a training perspective. The Craft is an experiential path, so it is important for the leader or teacher to facilitate the experiences in such a way that the student's process is not shorted out. Giving too much information ahead of time can prevent the student from having a genuine experience that they can own, so there are a few simple guidelines to adhere to.

Without being too specific – after all, you want to tailor this to your own practice – here are the guidelines I recommend:

1. Secrecy or Silence – the techniques and triggers of Visceral Magick should be withheld until the student has made a commitment to the group, as you need to have their word that they will not "spill the beans" to later students. The easiest way is an oath or promise of secrecy or silence, such as is often given at dedication or initiation.

2. Only provide enough information to allow the student to have the experience. Don't provide information about what to expect, but rather let them discover it for themselves, then talk about it afterward. This way, they take ownership of the experience and the understanding they receive, rather than having to take your word on it. This is why no one person can claim proprietary rights on the Mysteries, because we must all discover them for ourselves.

3. Every student is different – allow yourself the flexibility to take into account that one student might rush in with the barest of practical instruction, while another may need more instruction, and more discussion about the philosophical side. Just remember not to "give away the plot", and let the final experience be theirs.

4. Once they have had an experience, let them know who in the group has already had that experience, so they can talk with them. Many of these experiences only make sense after time and pondering, and the only people who they can safely discuss it with are those who have shared the experience.

5. Never forget that in the process of teaching or facilitating these experiences, it is likely that you will have new insights of your own. Never be afraid to learn from your students.

6. Every aspect of your tradition is an opportunity to work viscerally, from the symbols you use to the invocations and format of your rituals. Don't be afraid to explore every nut and bolt of your lore and practice. At the very least, you will gain a new perspective, and that is never a bad thing.

Initiation

*I*t will be no surprise that initiation is a key process when it comes to visceral magick. The inner initiation is an obvious focal point here, but the initiation into a coven or tradition can be done in such a way as to facilitate the process. Of course, this does require a few things that are very unpopular in the current Pagan community.

First of all, the idea of initiation itself is out of favor in some very vocal segments of the community. They see initiation as hierarchical and elitist, and want nothing to do with it. Of course, historically, initiation has more often been a personal thing between the practitioner and their gods, so on one level at least, they may have a point. And to be frank, many of the initiations that are given turn out to be ritual theater, with no fear of failure, and no real challenges. In other words, many groups make big noises about their initiations, and then they turn out to be little more than a formality, a rubber stamp that the candidate receives for merely walking along the path laid out before them.

A visceral initiation, whether it is a formal rite of passage or an inner experience, is never a formality. There is always a very real chance of failing the test, and the outcome is never certain. If it is a formal coven rite, there will be a moment of crisis that triggers the initiatory event, and this is the main reason why most initiations these days are simply walk-through, as this is dramatically politically incorrect, and is often misconstrued as abusive. But as long as the candidate is aware that the rite will be difficult and may be traumatic, and they consent as adults, this is no different legally to participating in the BDSM community. Ironically, there are many who endorse the BDSM lifestyle, yet scream long and loud at the idea of undergoing an initiation that they might fail. That is why this path is for the few, not the many.

It should also go without saying that not every student will make it to the point of initiation, let alone pass the rite itself. The teacher or coven leader is not going to put someone through the rite because they've "put in their time", because when an initiation rite fails, it is painful and traumatic for all participants, so the teacher will gauge when or if the student is ready to try, and whether they are likely to succeed. This can never be certain, though the teacher will do their best, for their own sake as well as the sake of the student.

The specifics of the rite itself will depend heavily on the symbolism and lore of the tradition the student is being initiated into, but the universal key points will always be the same for a shamanic/witchcraft initiation of the visceral variety. There will be a challenge at the entrance, followed by a ritual separating of the candidate from everything mundane, such as brushing them down with a besom. They will be brought, properly prepared (usually this means bound and blindfolded) into the center of the working space, and the entire group will then undertake a descent into the underworld, by whatever name it is known in the tradition. Here the first test is given, to ensure that the student is actually ready. Obviously I won't give specifics, but if the student is going to fail, this is the most common point where the failure occurs.

Once it is clear that the student is ready, then the rite proceeds to the main crisis point, where the candidate is truly tested at a deep and visceral level. Once again, I'm not going to spoil the surprise, but you can get a pretty good idea of what sort of thing occurs from reading some of the classical accounts of initiation – more is "hidden in plain sight" than you might expect, when it comes to the Mysteries.

Once the crisis has been passed, the candidate is mostly secure. The rest of the ritual is generally concerned with emotionally, spiritually and energetically linking the candidate to the group mind, egregore and "bloodline" of the group and tradition. This part can also fail, as the candidate may for some reason fail to "hook up" to the connections provided, in which case the initiation would still be technically a success from a personal perspective, but would not be a valid initiation into the tradition.

The Result of Awakening

So you might be asking yourself "what is the point of all this deep and meaningful stuff – what is it going to do for me?" Well, to be honest, I am still going through the process myself, but I can share what it has done for or to me so far...

First of all, since I started having visceral experiences that were triggered by the various techniques and events described previously, I have noticed that magick has become much more physical for me. When I started on my path, and for many years, my ability to sense magical or psychic energy was more akin to having as vague feeling that something was there, and working my own magick was a combination of half-sensed feelings and a lot of visualizing and wishful thinking.

I always wanted my visions, whether they were in ritual or during guided meditations, to be crystal clear and in full Technicolor, but I had to make do with smoky impressions that reminded me of watercolors that had been washed out by spilled water. I came to the conclusion that this was as good as it would ever be, and as I was getting fairly good results from my magick, decided not to let it bother me.

But now that has all changed. Working viscerally has made everything, as I said, much more physical. Instead of sensing magical energy as a faint and indeterminate "tingle", I get a full physical response, as if I was sensing electricity... the hairs on my arms stand up, I feel warmth, pressure, a wind running behind my knees and up my spine, and a static charge. I see the presence of sacred space as a blue-white syrupy "thickness" to the air, and while I am aware that I am not seeing them with my physical eyes, the Gods, Ancestors and other entities we work with are clearly and sharply seen.

On top of this, I am quite aware that physical "tells" are becoming much more common in my rituals. By this I mean flames burning abnormally bright and tall, even spiraling. My connection with the Ancestors, the River of Blood, and my Patron and Matron, have all become very tangible to me. I believe that when I do healing or ritual work for others, it is a lot easier for them to perceive or sense what I am doing as well. Certainly in my coven it has become much easier to trigger the visceral response in others.

I am pretty certain that this will continue to grow. My Ancestors have told me, and I firmly believe them, that visceral magick is the key to the Old School kind of magick that we read about in the tales of Merlin, Taliesin, and the other great magicians of antiquity. I am already working on techniques and lore connected with the Witches' Gaze – also known as the Evil Eye – and placing a Glamour on people, two "old school" techniques that seem to be very accessible right now. If it all works out, that may be what my next book is about!

Glossary

Amirgen White-knee
A famous and powerful Celtic Irish poet, credited as the author of the Cauldrons of Poesy.

Alderney Edge
A prominent ridge of land in Cheshire, England, where Arthur and his knights are said to be sleeping in a secret chamber, awaiting the call to aid Britain once again.

Ashridge
Forest in the British midlands, near Luton and Milton Keynes.

Awakening the Dragon
The Dragon is seen as the "animal" part of the human psyche, or its Underworld component, and the source of a traditional crafter's power. It has to be awakened to access the power, but tempered by the Crown or Higher Self. A rough western analogue of the Kundalini Serpent.

Bel
The Celtic Sun God.

Belli
Consort of the Sun God.

Beltaine

Fire Festival that traditionally takes place on May Day or May Eve.

Besom bridge

Using a traditional birch broomstick to bridge the "moat between sacred and mundane space."

Bilé Tree

Gaelic term for the World Tree.

Black Goddess

Black Annis, the dark Goddess who is unmanifest, and who is at once outside of the manifest universe and at its center. She is the Dark Twin of the White Goddess, and they are the two faces of Magick.

Black Sun

The Sun found in Celtic cosmology at the heart of the world. Source of the Forge Fire.

Blodeuwedd

The maiden created from flowers by Gwyddion and Math as a bride for Llew, to overcome his mother's final curse, that he would never marry a mortal bride.

Blood the Stone

In traditional witchcraft, oaths or promises are often solemnized by a drop of blood being placed on the central hearthstone, which is the focal point of the Ancestral Altar.

Bone immersed in the blood

This phrase refers to enfleshing the Lore by taking the Ancestral memories and lineage of the crafter and bringing them to life with the philosophy and practice of the tradition or path.

Bone ladder

Represents the Ancestors who came before. In modern terms, every initiate of the tradition who came before you, and on whose power and support you can draw.

Boyne

River in Ireland.

Cader Idris

A mountain in the Snowdonia range of Welsh mountains. Druid initiations were carried out on its summit, and the mountain curves around Lake Tegid Foel (now called Lake Bala), the home of Cerridwen. It is said in local lore that a man who spends the night on top of Cader Idris will greet the dawn either dead, mad or a poet. Named after Idris Gawr (Cader Idris literally means "chair of Idris"), the Welsh Giant who was patron of wisdom and learning.

Cauldron of Rebirth and the pearl-rimmed prototype of the Holy Grail, warmed by the breath of nine maidens

This is also known as the Cauldron of Cerridwen. In battle, slain warriors were revived by being placed in it. When we die, we are said to go into the Cauldron of Rebirth in order to be "recycled" and reborn.

Ced

The enclosure that contains the Black Sun, Mistress of the Mysteries.

Celli

The Dark Twin of Bel, the personification of the Black Sun at the heart of the World, and consort of Ced.

Cerridwen

Welsh Goddess, owner of the Cauldron of Rebirth.

Child of Promise

Term used for the potential all crafters have of manifesting the power and Mystery of the Sacred King cycle.

Cromh

"The Old Bent Blade", Cromh was a titanic deity in Celtic Ireland who was said to cause the sap to rise in plants and trees in spring from beneath the ground. There was a great God-Stone sacred to him at Tara, where children were sacrificed to him in ancient times. Enemy of Lugh.

Culhwch

The son of Cilydd son of Celyddon and Goleuddydd, a cousin of Arthur, who is aided by Mabon to gain the hand of Olwen in marriage.

Current

A magical Current is a group of traditions that are related by culture, pantheon or style of practice. For example, Thelema is a Current that consists of groups such as the OTO that derive their lore or inspiration from Aleister Crowley. All Celtic magical Paths could be considered part of the Celtic Current, though it branches into the Welsh, Irish, Scottish and Continental Currents.

Devil on your back

When entering the Wasteland, especially as part of an initiatory experience, it is sometimes found that the weight of your doubts, insecurities and worldly woes will manifest literally as the "Devil on your back", and it is necessary to confront this entity in order to move on. Similar to the concepts of the Dweller on the Threshold, and the Dark Night of the Soul.

Eber Donn

Chief of the Milesian invaders of ancient Ireland.

Elphame

Old English and Scottish name for the Faery realms.

Fisher King

Monarch of the Wasteland, Loegres in the Arthurian tales, with a wound in his thigh that would not heal until Sir Galahad used the Holy Grail to cure him, restoring health and vitality to the kingdom, which had wasted away along with the injured king.

Forge Flame

Fiery energy from the Black Sun at the heart of the World.

Forge-Fire

Fiery energy drawn up from the Great Forge, another term for the Black Sun perceived to be at the heart of the Earth.

Gronw

Gronw or Geronwy, is the enemy of Llew, and in many ways the Welsh equivalent of Cromh, as Llew is the Welsh equivalent of Lugh.

Gwion Bach

Literally "young lad", Gwion was the youth that Cerridwen set to tend the Cauldron containing the potion she intended for her son. Gwion inadvertently drank three drops of the potion, becoming filled with all wisdom, and after a series of initiatory transformations was reborn as Taliesin, the Greatest bard of Wales.

Hieros Gamos

The Sacred Marriage, or union of the King with the Goddess as personification of the Land. An act of sexual Mystery that bestows sovereignty upon the participants.

Holly King

One half of the traditional duo that represent the battle between Light and Dark, or Summer and Winter

Horned Lord

Ancient God of Witchcraft, also known as the Master of Magick, Lord of the Mound, and as Death.

Houzle

Cornish name for the libation of wine and cake in traditional craft, often done to honor the Horned Lord and the Ancestors.

Imbas

Poetic Frenzy – bards who entered the state of Imbas would speak poetically, often in tongues, and would manifest the will of the Gods.

Imbolc

Fire festival that takes place around the church festival of Candlemas.

Interior Sun

Another name for the Black Sun.

Knife's edge or glass bridge of Germanic myth

The bridge between the realms is often depicted as a knife-edge, or made of glass. It is often described as being found at the edge of a community, bridging a river that runs at the edge of a great forest.

Lammas

Fire Festival that takes place in early August, derives from "Loaf-Mass" from the old church calendar, and from Lugnasadh, the Irish Festival of Lugh.

Ley-line

Energy flow, often known as Dragon-Lines or the "Old Straight Track", or Faery-roads. Natural "rivers" of energy occurring throughout the world, detectable to sensitive people.

Llew

Llew Llaw Gyffes is a Welsh deity, who is the archetype for the Sacred King cycle. The son of Arianrhod and an unnamed father, he overcame the three curses of his mother, with the aid of her brother Gwyddion the Magician.

Lord of the Mound

The Horned Master of Magick, in his role as Lord of the Underworld, or Death.

Lore

The body of myth, poetry and wisdom held within a tradition or current.

Mabinogion

A collection of eleven Celtic Welsh stories, first translated into English by Lady Charlotte Guest from the White Book of Rhydderch and the Red Book of Hergest, both written in the 14th century.

Mabon, Son of Modron

Literally, "Son, Son of the Mother", Mabon is the template for the Hero's Journey in Welsh mythology.

Matron and Patron

Crafters who practice their art within a religious setting will usually have a God and Goddess who take on the role of tutelary deities. These are traditionally known as their Matron and Patron (Latin for "mother" and "father").

Nine hazels

In Irish Celtic mythology, the spring or well where the Salmon of Wisdom lives is surrounded by nine hazel trees that produce flowers and nuts at the same time. The nuts fall into the water, and the salmon feeds upon them.

Oak King

One half of the traditional duo that represent the battle between Light and Dark, or Summer and Winter.

Olwen

Daughter of the giant Yspaddaden Pengawr, whose hand in marriage is won by Culhwch with the aid of Mabon, Son of Modron.

Over the hedge

To jump over the hedge, or cross the moat is to journey between the worlds.

Path

A combination of the experience, journey and practice of an individual or small group of practitioners.

Preiddeu Annwn

The Welsh poem that describes the journey of King Arthur and his knights to the Nine Castyles of the Welsh Celtic Underworld, Annwn.

Puck

Mischievous spirit of nature, one of the lighter aspects of the Green Man.

Ride the dragon

A technique for harnessing the Underworld energies of our lower, or animal, self. Somewhat akin to raising Kundalini energy.

River of Blood

The flow of power, lore and magick that makes up the intangible component of a tradition or lineage.

Road to Elphame

A series of stories detailing the visits – usually accidental – of mortals to the Faery realms.

Robin Goodfellow

Common name for the spirit of nature often depicted as the Green Man.

Sacred King Cycle

In ancient times, a king would rule – or more accurately, serve the tribe or clan – for seven years before being sacrificed to the Gods. This was seen as an expression of the "slain and risen god" mysteries. In modern use, the cycle is worked as a year-long crafting, and usually involves the symbolic trials, death and rebirth of the god-king.

Salmon-leap

The Salmon Leap is the term applied in Irish Celtic mythology to the method of gaining access to the Isle of Skye, where the Warrior Goddess Scathach taught Celtic warriors the art of war. To prove themselves, the prospective students had to leap across the gap between the island and the mainland.

Samhain

All Hallow's Eve, the Celtic Fire Festival that celebrates the time when the veil between the worlds is thinnest.

Sidhe realm

The Sidhe are the Celtic Faery Folk, and the Sidhe Realm is where they exist – another name for Elphame.

Spindle

The heart of a spinning wheel, the spindle is often used as a metaphor for the World Tree, which is often described as spinning or rotating between the Worlds.

Stang

A forked stick that is used in traditional Witchcraft as the altar of the Horned God, frequently used to represent the World Tree in rituals. The fork can be a naturally forking branch, animal horns or the iron tines of a hay-fork, depending on the tradition.

Taliesin

Transformed by Cerridwen's potion, Taliesin was filled with all wisdom, becoming a great poet and prophet.

The language of the Gods is poetry

Robert Grave's book, "The White Goddess", puts forward the theory that poetry is the language of the gods.

Thomas The Rhymer

Also known as True Thomas, he is the protagonist of a traditional take about encountering the Faery realm. He meets a woman on a white horse, who turns out to be Queen of the Faeries, who keeps him in the Faery realms for seven years.

Toad Bone

A token or amulet obtained from a toad using a specific ritual procedure, that is said to confer upon the bearer mastery over animals along with magical power.

Trilithon

A "doorway" composed of two upright megaliths (big rocks) capped by a horizontal stone, as seen at Stonehenge.

Tyrch Trwth

The Great Boat slain by Mabon in his quest to prove himself and aid Culhwch gain the hand of Olwen in marriage.

Wayland's Smithy

A Neolithic long barrow and chamber tomb site located near the Uffington White Horse, said to be the home or workshop of Wayland Smith. He was said to have been given the task of making the nails for the crucifixion of Jesus, but one of the four refused to cool down, which is why Jesus was crucified with only three nails. As a penance, he is said to work at his forge every night, shoeing hoses that are left at the Smithy at sunset.

Well of Segais

The name of the well where the Salmon of Wisdom lives.

White Goddess

In traditional craft, there are two Goddesses of Magick. The White Goddess, sometimes referred to as "le Belle Grande Dame Sans Merci" (the Great Beautiful Lady without Mercy), is the Great Mother within manifest Creation. She can be equated to Isis from Ancient Egypt. Her dark sister is the Black Goddess, sometimes called Black Annis or Anna, who is seen as the Umnanifest, both outside of and at the center of Creation.

World Tree

The World Tree, or World Ash, is a great tree that is perceived as connecting the three realms of Celtic Cosmology, often referred to as Earth, Sea and Sky, or Heaven, Hell (the Underworld), and Here.

Bibliography

Davies, Sioned (trans.). The Mabinogion. New York: Oxford University Press, 2008.

Gershon, Michael. The Second Brain: A Groundbreaking New Understanding of Nervous Disorders of the Stomach and Intestine. New York: Harper Paperbacks, 1999.

Matthews, Caitlin. Arthur and the Sovereignty of Britain: King and Goddess in the Mabinogion. New York: Penguin, 1990.

Matthews, Caitlin. Mabon and the Guardians of Celtic Britain: Hero Myths in the Mabinogion. Rochester: Inner Traditions, 2002. [2nd edition]

Squire, Charles. Celtic Myth and Legend. Charleston: BiblioLife, 2009. [originally published 1912]

Stewart, R. J. Stewart and Bowers, Felicity. The Mystic Life of Merlin. New York: Penguin, 1988.

Index

A

B

C

D

E

I

J

K

L

ꟿ

ℕ

O

P

Q

R

S

T

Y

Lightning Source UK Ltd.
Milton Keynes UK
UKOW05f1956071116
287101UK00018B/980/P